KU-164-473

# Cytiau Chwain a Phalasau Breuddwydion

# Fleapits and Picture Palaces

Beth Thomas

Amgueddfeydd ac Orielau Cenedlaethol Cymru
National Museums & Galleries of Wales
1997

Dylunio a chynhyrchu: Arwel Hughes
Teip: New Baskerville 10/12pt
Argraffu: D. Brown a'i Feibion Cyf.
ISBN: 0 7200 0443 8



Design & production: Arwel Hughes
Type: New Baskerville 10/12pt
Printing: D. Brown and Sons Ltd.
ISBN: 0 7200 0443 8

Canmlwyddiant Ffilm
1896 - 1996
100 Years of Cinema

# Rhagarweiniad
# *Introduction*

Aeth canrif heibio ers i ni yng Nghymru weld ffilmiau symudol am y tro cyntaf. Dangoswyd y ffilmiau sinematograff cyntaf ym Mharis yn 1895 gan y brodyr Lumière. Cyn pen blwyddyn, daeth y dechnoleg newydd i Gymru, a thrwy ymdrechion glew arloeswyr fel William Haggar ac Arthur Cheetham a'u sioeau symudol, tyfodd y sinema yn rhan annatod o ddiwylliant poblogaidd y ganrif hon.

Dros y blynyddoedd bu Cymru yn llwyfan i ffilmiau; yn fagwrfan i actorion a chyfarwyddwyr byd enwog megis Emlyn Williams, Hugh Griffith, Richard Burton, ac Anthony Hopkins; ac yn fwy diweddar yn ganolfan gynhyrchu i'w ffilmiau safonol ei hun. Ond nid hanes enwogion yn unig yw hanes y sinema. Lawn mor bwysig yw profiad pobl gyffredin o fynd i'r sinema, yn enwedig yn y cyfnod hwnnw cyn dyfodiad y teledu, pan oedd y sinema yn fan cymdeithasu allweddol a'i dylanwad yn gryf ar ffasiynau ac agweddau yr oes.

Er protestio crefyddwyr mai 'synagog Satan' ydoedd, dihangfa o galedi eu bywydau beunyddiol oedd y sinema i Gymry ledled y wlad. Yma gellir darllen atgofion nifer o bobl am y dylanwad a gafodd y sinema arnynt, a'r cyffro o fynd i'r tywyllwch i wylio 'haul Holiwd'. Mae'r deunydd a gyflwynir yn gyfuniad o dystiolaeth lafar a gwybodaeth a ddaeth inni ar ffurf llythyrau. Lle bo'r dystiolaeth wreiddiol yn Gymraeg, darperir cyfieithiad, tra gadewir yr enghreifftiau Saesneg heb eu cyfieithu.

*A century has passed since Welsh audiences saw projected motion pictures for the first time. Less than seven months after the Lumière brothers first displayed their Cinématographe machine in Paris in 1895, the new technology had arrived in Cardiff. Through the pioneering efforts of Birt Acres and R.W. Paul, and the travelling shows of Arthur Cheetham and William Haggar, the cinema rapidly became an important influence on Welsh popular culture in this century.*

*Since those early days, hundreds of films have been shot in Wales; we have produced many men and women, from Ivor Novello to Antony Hopkins, who have made their names in the world of the cinema; and we have now developed a flourishing film and television industry of our own. Yet the history of the cinema is not just a matter of famous names. The cinema-going experiences of ordinary men and women are equally important, especially when we consider those pre-television days when the influence of the cinema on attitudes and fashion was at its height.*

*This book contains the cinema reminiscences of people from many parts of Wales, whose memories range from the days of the silent pictures (when the ability to read was a distinct advantage) to the immediate post-war years. The material is a combination of oral testimony and information sent to us by letter. Where the original testimony was recorded in Welsh, we have provided a translation; the English-language extracts have been left in their original language and idiom.*

# Rhagarweiniad
# *Introduction*

Hoffem ddiolch yn arbennig i BBC Cymru am adael inni ddefnyddio deunydd a recordiwyd ar gyfer y gyfres *All Our Lives*, a hefyd am sicrhau bod y tapiau ymchwil ar gyfer y gyfres honno ar gael i ddefnyddwyr archif sain yr Amgueddfa Werin. Rhaid diolch hefyd i Mici Plwm am rannu ffrwyth ei gasglu dyfal a'i wybodaeth am sinemâu yng Nghymru. Yn olaf oll, diolch o galon i'r holl unigolion a sefydliadau a restrir isod am gyfrannu at y prosiect, naill ai trwy fenthyg lluniau, neu drwy rannu eu profiadau ar lafar a thrwy lythyr. 'Rydym yn cydnabod unrhyw hawlfraint a all berthyn i'r defnyddiau hyn.

*We are especially indebted to BBC Wales for allowing us to use material recorded for the series* All Our Lives, *and for ensuring that the unedited interviews for that series are safely deposited for reference at the Museum of Welsh Life. Special mention must also be given to Mici Plwm for sharing his collection of Welsh cinema photographs and years of enthusiastic research. Finally we would like to thank all the individuals and institutions listed below for providing illustrations and photographs, or for sharing their experiences on tape or by letter. Any copyright that may exist in the material used is acknowledged by the Museum.*

**Gwybodaeth *Information:***

Arthur Austin, Paul Barrett, David Berry, Henry Burns, Jim Cowley, Bryn Davies, T.J. Davies, Tom Davies, Cora Edwards, Beryl Ellis, D.E. Griffiths, Mair Jones, Marian Jones, Peggy Jones, Marjorie Knowles, Eirwen Lewis, Eira Lloyd Crocombe, Emyr Owen, Peggy Page, J.E. Pugh, Hugh R. Jones, Eirona Richards, David Subacchi, Irene Thomas, Iris Roderick Thomas, R. Thomas, Vincent Thomas, Emlyn Williams, John E. Williams.

**Lluniau *Illustrations:***

Amgueddfa Castell Cyfarthfa / Cyfarthfa Castle Museum

Amgueddfa Brycheiniog / Brecknock Museum

Amgueddfa Ceredigion / Ceredigion Museum

Archifdy Penfro , Cyngor Sir Penfro / Pembrokeshire Record Office, Pembrokeshire County Council

Cardiff Yesterday

C.W. Beretta Casgliad T.J. Davies, Cwmgïedd Eric H. Chamberlain

Gwilym Hughes Dewi Jones Fred Jones Gareth T. Jones W.J. Kenny

Gwasanaeth Archif Sirol Gorllewin Morgannwg / West Glamorgan County Archive Service

The Kobal Collection Llyfrgell Caerdydd / Cardiff Central Library

Llyfrgell Cyngor Bwrdeisdref Sirol Wrecsam / Wrexham County Borough Council Library

Llyfrgelloedd Cyhoeddus Merthyr Tudful / Merthyr Tydfil Public Libraries

Mrs Ruth Morris Mici Plwm Harry Thomas Mrs R. Thomas Huw Walters

Valleys Arts Marketing

CYNNWYS - *CONTENTS*

Ffair Aberhonddu, Powys, tua 1915.
Buasai'r sinematograff, gyda'i luniau symudol o'r rhyfel, yn atyniad mawr.

*Brecon Fair, Powys, c.1915,*
*The cinematograph bringing moving pictures of the war would have been a major attraction.*

# Wele Dechnoleg Wyrthiol!
## *A Miraculous Technology!*

GRAND ENTERTAINMENT OF

**Cinematograph Pictures.**

*The best obtainable.* *Direct from London.*

AFTERNOON AND EVENING PERFORMANCES.

PICTURES CHANGED THREE TIMES WEEKLY,
MONDAYS, WEDNESDAYS, AND SATURDAYS.

Admission–3d and 6d.

CHILDREN'S MATINEE EVERY SATURDAY AFTERNOON at 3 o'clock.

Admission–1d.

THEATRE OPEN AT 2 AND 7 O'CLOCK. No Extra Charge for Early Doors.

*This wonderful instrument is one of the great inventions of the age... It may be described as an adaptation of the Kinetoscope and the Magic Lantern, enabling the audience to witness upon a screen on which the light is thrown the movements of a crowd or of individual persons... The performance was a remarkable success and all present declared themselves astonished with the series of pictures thrown upon the screen.*
*South Wales Echo*, 6/5/1896

**Disgrifiad o'r perfformiad Kineopticon cyntaf yn Arddangosfa Celfyddyd Gain, Diwydiant a Môr Caerdydd**

***An account of the first Kineopticon performance at the Cardiff Fine Art, Industrial and Maritime Exhibition.***

Arferion sydd wedi llygru moesau'r wlad yw mynychu'r Picture Palaces a'r Cinemas, a'r dras cyffelyb,... y mae hyd yn oed y Ddrama Gymraeg mewn rhai achosion yn disgyn i bethau sydd yn ddiamheuol gabledddus a llygredig.

*Habits which have corrupted the morals of the country are the frequenting of Picture Palaces and Cinemas and similar places... even the Welsh Drama in some cases has sunk to matters that are undoubtedly blasphemous and corrupt.*

**M.M. John, Trecynon, yn *Y Darian*, 4/3/1915**

Fe fyddem ni'n gweld rhyfeddodau ac anturiaethau, chwedlau gwerin cyfareddol yr ugeinfed ganrif - yn Saesneg i gyd, wrth gwrs. Ond yr adeg honno, roedd Cymraeg y gymdeithas yn ddigon cryf i droi'r rhan fwyaf o'r estron bethau a ddeuai i'n byd ni yn bethau Cymraeg.

*We would witness marvels and adventures, the magical folk tales of the twentieth century - all in English, of course. But in those days, the Welsh of the community was strong enough to transform most of the foreign elements that came into our world into things that were Welsh.*

***Yn Blentyn yn y Blaenau*, Gwyn Thomas, 1981**

Sinema deithiol William Haggar, tua 1900. Roedd Haggar yn un o arloeswyr mawr y sinema yng Nghymru, yn gwneud ei ffilmiau ei hun yn ogystal â chodi sinemâu ar draws y de.

*William Haggar's Royal Electric Bioscope, c. 1900. Haggar was one of the greatest pioneers of cinema in Wales, making his own films as well as setting up cinemas all over South Wales.*

# Wele Dechnoleg Wyrthiol!
*A Miraculous Technology!*

Dangoswyd lluniau symudol yn fasnachol yng Nghymru am y tro cyntaf yn yr Empire, Stryd y Frenhines, Caerdydd, 1896.

*The first commercial screening in Wales of projected moving pictures was at the Empire Theatre, Queen Street Cardiff, 1896.*

NEXT WEEK!!

AT

THE EMPIRE

Once Again at Great Expense,

THE ORIGINAL . .
. . UNSURPASSED . .
. . UNEQUALLED

. LUMIERE .

CINEMATOGRAPHI

From the Empire, London,

Under the Direction of M. TREWEY.

A Series of Brilliant and Interesting Scenes absolutely true to life
PRECISION, PROPORTION AND MOTION.

Towerskay in Moscow.
Children—Cat and Dog.
The Disappointed Artist.
Burmese Dance at the Crystal Palace.
Hamburg Bridge, Germany.
Soldiers' Parade in Madrid.
Concorde Bridge, Paris.
Lancers in Stuttgart.
Artillery in Barcelona.
Fire Brigade Call, London.
Charge of Cavalry in France.

AND

A Remarkable Picture—"TOBOGGANING IN SWITZERLAND."

You would have to expend a large amount of money and time to obtai view of the Scenes of the above Programme in their Geographical situation, by the aid of this wonderful instrument in conjunction with Motor Photograp they are brought before you exact in form and motion for the money and tim visit to the Empire entails

Tudor Printing Works, Cardiff.

# Wele Dechnoleg Wyrthiol!
## *A Miraculous Technology!*

Pafiliwn adloniant Edwards & Page, lle gwelodd T.J. Davies ei luniau symudol cyntaf, ar sgwâr Ystradgynlais, Powys. Erbyn 1918, roeddent wedi adeiladu sinema barhaol foethus yn y dref.

*Edwards & Page's Picture Pavilion, where T.J. Davies saw his first moving pictures, at Ystradgynlais Square, Powys. By 1918 they had built a permanent and luxurious cinema in the town.*

*It was, more or less, at the birth of the cinema. I should say it was 1914... They were real pioneers in the true sense of it. They brought [the pavilion] down to Ystradgynlais and they erected it in the yard in front of Ynyscedwyn Arms and it stayed there until they built the new cinema. It was Edwards and Page. They travelled under that particular name.... The first thing I can remember about the cinema on the square, they had this musical front - the organ, marionettes or whatever they were. [It was] the first time I ever went in and probably the last time because my granny was very self righteous and godly and all that. Oh! you were following the devil when you'd go to the pictures then! It was like a fairground - and the huge marquee! It had been raining and you had duckboards underfoot, and the only thing I can remember vividly - why, I don't know - was this Red Indian crawling up this brook or river and chasing somebody and he had a huge dagger in his mouth. I can see him now.*

**T.J. Davies, Cwmgïedd, Powys, ganed / born 1907**

# Lluniau Mud
## *Silent Movies*

Odd y sinema yn dod yn ail i'r capel, weden i. Odd y sinema yn *wonderful*. Yn yr amser ŵ i'n sôn, odd llwmdra ofnadw. Odd lot o bobol yn ddi-waith. A'th gwrs, am ddwy ginog och chi'n gallu mynd i'r sinema, naill ne *Hall* y Cwm, ne Shew Sam - ne Shanti Sam odd rai'n galw fe. Ddim llawer o filding, ond ôn ni'n mynd 'na. A'r amser wi'n cofio ginta odd y *silent pictures*. Odd ddim siarad o gwbwl - odd y sgrifen yn dod mâs ar y sgrîn, a pobun - fi'n gallu gweld y plant nawr - yn darllen y peth yn dod mâs ar y sgrîn. A ryw *hum* o'r llishe bach yn darllen. Ond beth odd yn bwysig iawn yn amser y *silent films* odd y piano. Y piano odd yn rhoi y *mood*. Os odd rwbeth bach trist - gwedwch bod gwidw'n câl 'i thwlu mâs o'i thŷ gan y dyn drwg odd yn ffilu câl 'i ffordd gida'i, ys gwedon nw - we'ny bydde'r piano'n gweud 'Dy dy dy, dy dy dy dy,' a'r plant i gyd yn bŵan ag yn *hiss*an y *villain* chimod. Wed'ny os bydde'r cowbois ne rwbeth bach mwy cyffrous, bydde'r piano'n ware 'Bymp papa rym papa rym papa rym.' Plant yn stampo ag yn clapo. Chimod, nagodd plant mor *sophisticated* pry'ny â ma nw nawr, wi ddim credu! Och chi'n roi *vent* i'ch teimlade'n fwy.

*The cinema came second to chapel, I would say. The cinema was wonderful. In the period I'm talking about, there was a lot of poverty. A lot of people were unemployed. And of course, for tuppence you could go to the cinema, either to the Hall in the Cwm, or to Sam's Show - or Sam's Shanty as some called it. Not much of a building, but we went there. And my earliest memory is of the silent pictures. There was no talking at all. The words would come out on the screen and everyone would be - I can see the children now - reading what appeared on the screen. And the little voices reading made a kind of a hum. But in the time of silent films, the piano was very important. It was the piano that set the mood. If there was something sad - say a widow being thrown out of her home by the wicked man who couldn't have his way with her, as they say - the piano would play 'Da da da, da da da da' and the children would all boo and hiss at the villain. Then if there were cowboys or something a bit more exciting, the piano would play 'Bum pappa rum, pappa rum, pappa rum'. And the children would stamp and clap. You know, I don't think children were as sophisticated then as they are today. They gave more vent to their feelings.*

**Mrs Peggy Jones, Brynaman, Sir Gaerfyrddin/ Carmarthenshire, ganed / born 1921**

Neuadd y Dref, Pwllheli, Gwynedd yn llawn gwylwyr sinema, tua 1910.

*Standing room only at a cinema performance in the Town Hall, Pwllheli, Gwynedd c.1910.*

# Lluniau Mud
## *Silent Movies*

Siop gig ym Mrynaman, Sir Gaerfyrddin, yn yr 1920au, gyda phosteri yn hysbysebu sinema'r Alpha yn y ffenestr

*A butcher's shop at Brynaman, Carmarthenshire, in the 1920s, with posters advertising the Alpha cinema in the window*

Roedd y pictiwrs yn cael eu dangos yn y *Public Hall*. Fe gostiai ddwy geiniog am fynediad. *5pm matinee* pnawn Sadwrn. Cyn i'r *talkies* ddŵad, llynia du a gwyn, gyda'r geiriau yn ymddangos ar waelod y lluniau. Y piano yn cael ei chwarae gan y diweddar Arthur Alun Jones, a chwarae yn gyflym fel oedd angen i gyfartalu â'r llun.

*Pictures were shown in the Public Hall. It used to cost tuppence to go in. 5pm matinee Saturday afternoon. Before the talkies came, it was black and white pictures with the words appearing across the bottom. The piano would be played by the late Arthur Alun Jones, and he'd play faster to go along with the picture.*

**Emlyn Williams, Rachub, Bangor, Gwynedd**

*Mrs Templeman would be there playing, and there'd be no speaking, it would just come up underneath like* Pobol y Cwm *do. She'd be there playing, wobbling on this old piano stool. But we could never understand why you had to have music playing while the picture was on. You were trying to watch the picture and she'd make this rattling noise on the piano that was like the horses coming... I don't suppose many kids can remember silent films... My youngest brother couldn't read [the captions] and he used to say,'What they saying now?' 'Oh, shut up! If you went to school you would be able to know what they were saying. You'd be able to read!'*

**Mrs Peggy Page, Oakdale, Caerffili, ganed / born 1924**

# Lluniau Mud
## *Silent Movies*

*The old gentlemen and the old ladies used to get down in the front, and if you were looking for a seat, a voice from the dark would say, 'Can you read?' And of course as a kid you were always trying to show off, and you're bound to say yes. They'd sit you along side of them - it was all silent pictures, of course - and you had to read what was on [the screen] when it came up: 'Don't darken my doors again!' I wouldn't be the only one, everyone else had to read with them, you know. 'Don't darken my doors again!...Three months later.' And of course three months later she was always having a baby - 'Ah, father forgive me!' Everyone was doing this, and the piano was playing like hell, especially the battle scenes. If there were cowboys going, they'd be belting away. And if there was anything naughty happening, you'd see one of these fellows dressed up like an officer or something, he'd pick up this young lady and they'd go into her room and the waves would come. I don't know where they got the waves from. There wasn't a ripple before, but now the wind and the rain would be lashing. You had an idea in your head that there was something that they didn't really want to show you, and then there'd be 'After the storm,' and of course we'd all be saying it. It was showing off, really, but the piano player would be there, belting away.*

**Henry Burns, Caerdydd / Cardiff. Ganed / Born 1916**

*Norma Talmadge and Rudolph Valentino in* The Sheik *were the excitements then, enhanced by the not infrequent breakdowns at the most thrilling part. We still waited outside in rain or shine for first or second house, sometimes being allowed in a few at a time as earlier patrons came out or, if the film warranted it, only being allowed in during the official break. Once in the foyer boyfriends joined another queue at the sweet and cigarette kiosk to buy a one shilling box of Needler's chocolates if you were lucky, otherwise a packet of boiled sweets. Rattling papers were not an annoyance then as one read the screen for the dialogue. But readers out loud were to be avoided at all costs.*

**Marjorie Knowles, Llandrindod, Powys**

Picture Palace, Troed-y-rhiw, Merthyr Tudful, 1929

George Edwards Hall.

**Stanley's Kinema, Cefn.**

Coming to Thrill and Astonish You!

COMMENCING MONDAY, NOV. 10th, AND THE FOLLOWING 3 or 4 DAYS.

A JAMES CRUZE PRODUCTION,

Presented by

ADOLPH ZUKOR & JESSIE L. LASKY,

# THE COVERED WAGON

By EMERSON HOUGH.

**The Greatest Success in the History of Pictures.**

Featuring

LOIS WILSON & J. WARREN KERRIGAN

Allan Hale, Charles Ogle, Ethel Wales, Ernest Torrence, Tully Marshall, Guy Oliver and John Fox.

**The Greatest International Success of the Century. The picture the whole country's talking about.**

**Just Imagine This**—YOU'LL SEE hundreds of men, women, children, horses, oxen—a two-mile wagon train of pioneer days—fleeing for their lives from a raging fire that laid waste nine miles of prairie. YOU'LL SEE a thousand real, yelling, painted Indians riding madly to attack in their famous "circle of death" formation. YOU'LL SEE a buffalo hunt with the world's only remaining herd of buffalo. YOU'LL SEE the wagon-train ford a turbulent mile wide torrent. YOU'LL SEE the whole spectacular heart-drama of the perilous, glorious days of '49. The story of a man's love and sacrifice for a beautiful girl in the most amazing settings ever photographed. Your most gorgeous screen adventure.

No Theatre has yet been able to accomodate all the patronage THE COVERED WAGON has inspired.

☛ **2 Shows Daily at 6 & 8.**

Matinee Wednesday at 3 o'clock.

**Prices: 4d., 6d., 1/-** including Tax.

Be advised - Book Early - open daily. Special shows for school children.

Hysbyseb ar gyfer ffilm fud yn *Stanley's Kinema*, Cefn, ger Wrecsam, 1924

*An advertisement for a silent picture showing at Stanley's Kinema, Cefn, near Wrexham, 1924.*

# Lee's Pictures, Amlwch

**Week commencing August 29th.**

Doors open 7-0. To commence at 7-30.

**Monday:**

**"MEET THE PRINCE."**

The story of a prince who set out to earn a living as a Butler. Be sure you meet the prince at the Cinema. You will be charmed.

OWING TO ENORMOUS SUCCESS

**Mr. FREDERICK DRUMMOND, the famous Composer**

will preside at the Piano and render special music. For this (Monday) night only.

**Wednesday:**

**"SILKEN SHACKLES"** FEATURING **IRENE RICH**

A WARNER CLASSIC that you must not miss. Life in Society and Diplomatic Circles. Also full programme.

**Thursday:**

**"MY OLD DUTCH"**

immortalised by the late ALBERT CHEVALLIER.

FOR THIS NIGHT ONLY

**Mr. HAROLD DOBBS (Bangor),**

the famous Pianist and Organist will preside at the Piano and render selections from the classics during the showing of this super picture.

Book your Seats now. No extra charge.

**Saturday:**

**"PRISONERS OF THE STORM"**

by JAMES OLIVER CURWOOD.

A Universal Special that will hold the audiences spellbound. This picture has run for a whole season in London. Don't miss it.

**Thursday and Saturday:**

**Serial: 'POLICE PATROL' and special Comedy.**

Saturday only, TWO HOUSES, 6-0 and 8-0.

Children first House only. Busses leave for all parts after First House.

| Admission: | 6d. | 9d. | 1s. |
|---|---|---|---|
| (...ding Tax) | Children 4d. | Children, 5d. | Children 6d. |

Hysbyseb ar gyfer Lee's Pictures, Amlwch, Ynys Môn, yn yr 1920au. Sylwer ar y cyfeiriadau at berfformiadau cerddorol.

*A 1920s advert for Lee's Pictures, Amlwch, Ynys Môn. Note the references to musical performances.*

Ddechrïes i ar y piano yn un ar ddeg. Yn bomtheg ôd geso i'r A.L.C.M. 'Na gyd odd 'y mywyd i odd miwsic a piano a whare gwahanol. Yn y gîa on i'n ware bob nos i bethach - côr capel, côr meibion. A wedi 'ny on i'n ware yn Isgol Sul, wth gwrs. Geso i amser bishi iawn ond ...[y gwinidog], amser glywodd e bo fi'n whare sinema, odd e'n gweud 'Ma bobol yn y capel hyn â talent yn neud sop o waith am arian!' ... Nagon i'n ito beth odd e'n gweud! On i'n mwynhau y gwaith. I weud y gwir 'thoch chi, ddisges i ddarllen miwsic. Geso i ddim trafferth byth i ddarllen miwsic. On i'n goffod neud e. On i'n câl lot o sbort. On i'n dishgwl lan ar y llun amser on i'n whare piano fan hyn a gweld Pearl White falle yn y dŵr a'r *octopus* chi'n gwbod â'r *tentacles* rownd iddi... A wedi 'ny wi'n cofio un tro odd *galloping horses*, chi'n gwbod, a on i'n gwbod bod miwsic lan yn yr *ante room* so on i'n rasan lan i gâl y miwsic nawr i siwto! On i'n goffod câl y miwsic i fynd gyda'r llun.

*I started playing piano at eleven. At fifteen years of age I got my A.L.C.M. Music and piano were my whole life. In the winter I used to play for something every night - chapel choir, male voice choir. And I played in the Sunday School, of course. I had a very busy time, but when the minister heard that I was playing in the cinema, he used to say, 'There are talented people in this chapel doing a lot of work for money!'...I didn't care what he said! I enjoyed the work. To tell you the truth I learnt to read music. I had to. We had a lot of fun. I'd look up at the picture while I was playing and I'd see Pearl White maybe in the water with octopus' tentacles round her... And I remember once there were galloping horses, and I knew that there was music up in the ante room, so I raced up to get suitable music! We had to have the music to go with the picture.*

**Cyn-bianydd yn sinema'r Alpha Brynaman, Sir Gaerfyrddin, ganed 1908**

**Former pianist at the Alpha Cinema, Brynaman, Carmarthenshire, born 1908**

# Lluniau Mud
## *Silent Movies*

Cerddorfa sinema'r Rink, Wrecsam, 1911.
*The orchestra of the Rink Cinema, Wrexham, 1911*

*Everything was timed on our music, you see? Each member of the orchestra had it timed. But the main thing was to follow the head violinist, or sometimes it was the conductor. Perhaps it'd be cowboys now, and you'd have very quick music and all that business. Well you'd perhaps repeat that section four times. You couldn't rely on what you had in your music. You had to keep your eye now on the conductor, simply because the operator would go faster, and he shouldn't. Well after that, perhaps somebody'd be dying, somebody'd fall off a horse. Well now, 'twas no good us playing fast music when this person would be dead, you see? It was really funny, mind. Uncle Sid was to the second! He had his eye up there - wonderful memory for music - he'd look up - Right, he's fallen off! And he was accurate!... I went to Aberystwyth to the college and worked in the silent films in the night. I was seventeen and that was in 1927, when I left Morriston. I was playing in the cinema in the night and college in the day, and that again was a marvellous combination. Everybody went to the college from there you know, the musicians, two fiddles, cello and piano, and we used to play high brow stuff. People used to go to listen to the music and not the film.*

**Miss Marian Jones, Treforys, Abertawe, ganed 1910. Cyn dyfod lluniau llafar, enillai teulu Miss Jones fywoliaeth trwy chwarae yn sinemâu a chyngherddau'r cylch.**

**Miss Marian Jones, Morriston, Swansea., born 1910. Before the advent of the 'talkies', Miss Jones' family earned their livelihood by playing in cinema orchestras and chapel concerts.**

## Lluniau Llafar
## *Talking Pictures*

Wedi'ny, fe ddâth y *talking pictures*. A odd e'n peth trist iawn i rai odd yn ware piano. Wi'n gwbod am un dyn lan yn Gwm Tawe, fe gomitws e *suicide*! Gollws e'i jobyn chwel. Odd dim lle iddo fe nawr ragor, a odd dim byd 'da fe neud... Ond i ni, pan ddâth y *talkies* odd e'n beth cyffrous ofnadw! Yr un ginta wi'n cofio odd - wi'n credu ta'r enw odd naill *Sunny Side Up* ne *If I had a Talking Picture of You*. Janet Gaynor a Charles Farrell odd yn acto nw. A chimod, am wthnose wedyn ôn ni'n

mynd rown Garnant a Glanaman yn canu *If I had a talking picture of you-hou*! Sdim llais 'ta fi ganu llawer nawr ond odd un bach arall - *Keep your sunny side up, up, Hide the side that gets blue. If you've eleven sons all in a row, football teams make money you know. So keep your sunny side up...* A'dd e'n diweddu rwbeth fel 'yn: *Stand upon your legs, be like two fried eggs. Keep your sunny side up.* Chimbod, *we'd laugh at it now, wouldn't we?* Fydden ni'n câl sbri ar 'i ben e. Ond ôn ni'n canu fe!

*Then the talking pictures came. And it was a sad thing for those who played the piano. I know of one man in the Swansea Valley who committed suicide! He'd lost his job, you see. There wasn't a place for him anymore, and he had nothing to do... But for us, it was an awfully exciting thing when the talkies came. The first one I remember was, I think, either* Sunny Side Up *or* If I Had a Talking Picture of You. *Janet Gaynor and Charles Farrell were the actors. And do you know, for weeks after that we went round Garnant and Glanaman singing 'If I had a talking picture of you-hou!' I haven't got much of a singing voice now but there was another one - 'Keep your sunny side up, up. Hide the side that gets blue. If you've eleven sons all in a row, football teams make money, you know. So keep your sunny side up...' And it finished something like this: 'Stand upon your legs, be like two fried eggs. Keep your sunny side up.' You know, we'd laugh at it now, wouldn't we? But we used to sing it!*

**Mrs Peggy Jones, Brynaman, Sir Gaerfyrddin/ Carmarthenshire, ganed / born 1921**

*Then came the 'Talkies' in about 1931. I well remember the tremendous intake of breath as Al Jolson sang 'Sonny Boy' when the picture was half way through, adding to the drama of the new invention of being heard for the first time.*

**Mrs Marjorie Knowles, Llandrindod, Powys**

*It was one of my earliest recollections, really, because I remember the day I came home from school. My mother was dressed up - they always dressed up in their best, you see, to go everywhere - and my mother had a hat on and her best coat and she said 'We're going to the cinema today. We're going to see Al Jolson in* The Singing Fool.*' And that was my first trip to the cinema. It was in the Castle Cinema, Merthyr Tydfil... and the queue, my goodness me, it was right round the corner! There were two queues actually. There was queues for the best seats which were a shilling; one and three up in the circle, which was only two rows; and the other queue of course was stretching right up the town and that was for the sixpennies and the ninepennies. But my mother said we'd go to the shillings, so we went to the circle. And I remember that we went a little bit late actually because it was a continuous show... and of course all the people that had gone in previously wouldn't come out! They wanted to see the film over again. So we all stood in the queue, and there was the commissionaire... He was a right character and he was standing there in the middle of the steps, you see, because there was a queue this side and a queue that side. He'd shout 'Two for the one and threes please! Four for the shillings!' And then he'd change his voice, 'Six ninepennies!' His voice changed according to the prices. Then we went in to see it. I don't think we'd been there more than about half an hour when everyone in the cinema was crying pints! Because he was singing* Sonny Boy*, you see. Al Jolson, his little boy had died, and he was saying 'Climb upon my knee, Sonny Boy'. Everybody was dripping tears, and I thought I don't want to go here again. But of course the next time I went it was a funny film. It was a Claudette Colbert film.*

**Mrs Iris Roderick Thomas, Merthyr Tudful, ganed / born 1927**

LEE'S TALKIE PICTURES,
AMLWCH.

WEEK COMMENCING FEBRUARY 29th.
TWO HOUSES NIGHTLY, 6-0 and 8-0.

MONDAY AND TUESDAY:
COUNT TOLSTOY'S MASTERPIECE
"RESURRECTION"
*featuring* JOHN BOLES.
THE CAST INCLUDES
Nance O'Neil and Lupe Valex the great Singer.
Banned from Love—Forbidden to marry and sent to prison for a crime she did not commit—This is one of the world's greatest Dramas—Now brought to the Talking and Singing Screen.
DON'T MISS IT.

WEDNESDAY AND THURSDAY:
'THE SEA BAT'
A ROMANCE OF THE SOUTHERN SEAS
Humour, Thrills, Gorgeous Scenery, a cast of Stars, including Raquel Torres, Charles Bickford, Nils Arthur, Mack Swain, etc.
This is a Metro Goldwyn super. Dont miss it.

FRIDAY AND SATURDAY:
'BIRDS OF PREY'
This is a mystery thriller and has a cast of 8 famous Stars including Dorothy Boyd, Warwick Ward, Aubry Smith etc, etc.
Supported by a screaming comedy.

Prices of Admission (including Tax)

| 1/2 | 9d. | 7d. |
|---|---|---|

MATINEE Saturday at 2-30.
Children 2d., 4d. & 5d. Adults 7d. to best Seats.
(ALL INCLUDING TAX).

Bus every night after pictures to Cemaes and Llanfechell, and Train every night after first house to Llanerchymedd.

# Cofion Cyntaf
## *First Encounters*

*I can still remember the feeling of, well, not exactly excitement, because we went to the pictures nearly every week, but definitely anticipation, when my mother would say, 'We're going to the pictures tonight. Don't be late for tea!' For a start, it was a family outing. Both my mother and my grandmother loved being entertained: my grandfather had been a notable singer and choir master when sober, and my mother often told us stories of growing up during the first world war and taking part in amateur dramatics in the Church Hall. Many of our friends never went to the cinema at all, but we went as a family. Dad was away at sea, but Mamgu, Mam, John and I walked the mile from Llanbadarn Fawr to Aberystwyth nearly every week. Buses were few and far between, and so, in an age when everyone walked everywhere, we saved the twopence to buy an ice-cream in the interval or sweets to take in.*

**Mrs Beryl Ellis, ganed / born Aberystwyth, Ceredigion**

*The old cinema in Llanrwst was a grey stone faced building in the street leading from Denbigh St. down to what was the Council school, a building which seemed cavernous to a child. I was taken to see films that were either adaptations of books or were regarded as of interest to a fairly widely read child. Sadly, I can only remember three visits, first to see* Ben Hur *from which I retain clear images of the chariot race and a triumphal procession; second to see* Palnell, *which so saddened me that I was swept from the cinema in floods of tears and lastly* The Hunchback of Notre Dame *of which I can only recall the jeering shouting crowd as the hunchback climbed.*

**Mrs Irene Thomas**

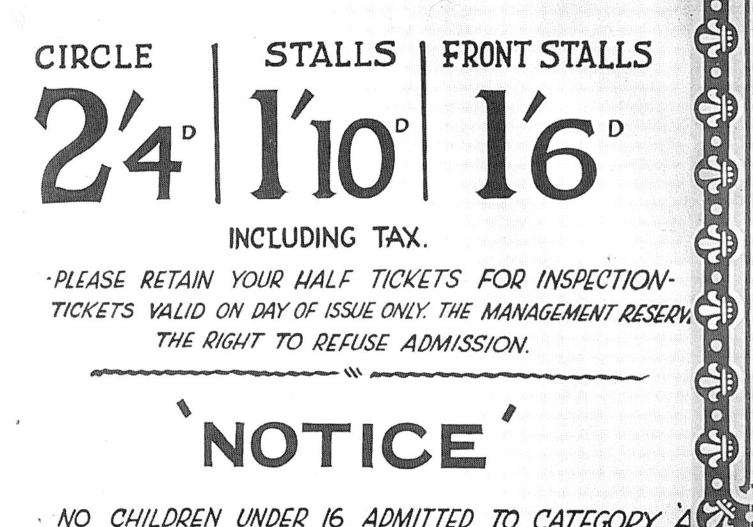

CIRCLE 2/4D | STALLS 1/10D | FRONT STALLS 1/6D

INCLUDING TAX.

·PLEASE RETAIN YOUR HALF TICKETS FOR INSPECTION·
TICKETS VALID ON DAY OF ISSUE ONLY. THE MANAGEMENT RESERV[E]
THE RIGHT TO REFUSE ADMISSION.

'NOTICE'

· NO CHILDREN UNDER 16 ADMITTED TO CATEGORY 'A'
FILMS UNLESS ACCOMPANIED BY AN ADULT.

COLISEUM
SUPER CINEMA
TERRACE ROAD, ABERYSTWYTH
CONTINUOUS from 6 to 10-30
MATINEE SATURDAY AT 2-30
Commencing MONDAY, SEPTEMBER 18
ALL THE WEEK!
A GREAT COMEDY
RALPH LYNN & WINIFRED SHOTTER
IN
JUST MY LUCK
EAST OF FIFTH AVENUE
THE YOUNG BRIDE
AMAZING ROYLETS
Owing to the length of Programme
WE START AT 6 O'CLOCK EACH NIGHT. Doors Open 5-30
PRICES: 1/3, 1/-, 9d. and 7d.
Children's Matinees 4d. and 7d.

Coliseum, Aberystwyth, 1930au / 1930s

*I was born in Aberystwyth in 1955 and my first memory of the cinema is leaving the Pier Cinema in tears with my parents. I remember little about the film except that it was in black and white and involved a battle but I was scared by the darkness and the vivid images on screen. I believe the Pier Cinema closed in the early 1960s so I could have been no older than four or five at the time.*
**David Subacchi, ganed / born Aberystwyth, Ceredigion, 1955**

*I think my interest in cinema started [in] the very early 50s and finding a film annual in a jumble sale. There was a film featuring a western character called the Darango Kid, who was dressed all in black and he had a black kerchief. I thought he looked great and I liked that. Of course, then there were two cinemas in Penarth. There was the Windsor Cinema in Windsor Road, and there was the Washington Cinema. So yeah, I started going to the cinema then and was hooked.*
**Paul Barrett, Penarth, Bro Morgannwg / Vale of Glamorgan, ganed / born 1941**

Posteri sinema, 1930au cynnar.
***Cinema posters, early 1930s.***



Palladium, Prestatyn, 1947

# Plaza, Forum, Empire...

Yn y tridegau a thrwy flynyddoedd y rhyfel, roedd gan dref Blaenau Ffestiniog dri o sinemâu. Y cyntaf un i ddangos ffilmiau sain oedd yr Empire, ar y Stryd Fawr. Yna yn ddiweddarach adeiladwyd Sinema'r Parc, neu'r *Park Cinema* yn ôl Cymry'r dref. Yn olaf adeiladwyd y Forum... Un tro penderfynodd sinema'r Empire ddangos ffilm a oedd wedi ei chynhyrchu ar gyfer y sgrîn fawr lydan. Ond och! Yr un maint oedd y sgrîn hon ag ar gyfer ffilmiau 35mm! Roedd y canlyniad yn ddoniol dros ben - y ffilm dan sylw oedd *Storm Over the Nile*, addasiad arall (ddim yn hollol gystal â'r un gwych o 1939) o nofel A.E.W. Mason *The Four Feathers*. Pan oedd y ffilm yn mynd trwy'r peiriant taflunio, gwelwyd milwyr Kitchener yn rhedeg fel y diawl o gyfeiriad y ffenestr ar y chwith, ar draws y sgrîn wreiddiol, ac yna yn erlid dynion drwg y Swdan reit allan drwy'r ffenestr ar y dde! Sôn am guro traed a dwylaw, a chrochlefain y plant yn y seddau blaen! Wele yma dechnoleg wyrthiol! Dywedwyd bod un boi wedi mynd allan drwy'r cefn er mwyn rhoi clustan neu ddwy i'r dynion drwg - oedd erbyn hyn siŵr o fod yn strydoedd cefn yr Empire, neu efallai yn carlamu ar draws sgrîn y Forum!

*In the thirties and throughout the war years, Blaenau Ffestiniog had three cinemas. The first to show talkies was the Empire, on the High Street. Later the Park Cinema was built, and finally the Forum... On one occasion the Empire decided to show a film that had been made for the wide screen. But oh! The screen was no bigger than that used for 35mm films. The consequences were extremely funny - the film was* Storm over the Nile, *another adaptation (not quite as good as the excellent 1939 version) of A.E.W. Mason's novel* The Four Feathers. *As the film passed through the projector, Kitchener's soldiers were seen running like the devil from the window on the left, crossing the original screen, and chasing the baddies from the Sudan right out of the window on the right! Talk about clapping and stamping of feet, and the shouting of the children in the front row! This was miraculous technology! It is said that one chap ran out the back to fight the bad men that were by now surely in the back lanes of the Empire, or perhaps galloping across the screen of the Forum!*

**Emyr Owen, Blaenau Ffestiniog, Gwynedd**

Sinema'r Forum, Blaenau Ffestiniog, Gwynedd a agorwyd tua 1934.
*The Forum Cinema, Blaenau Ffestiniog, Gwynedd, opened c. 1934.*

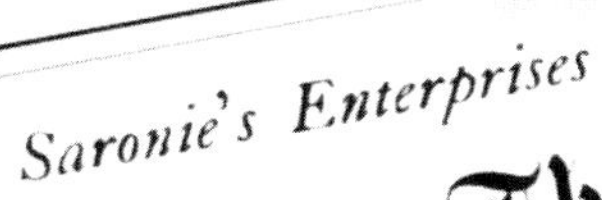

Saronie's Enterprises

# The Plaza Theatre and Super Cinema

HIGH STREET - - BANGOR

The Most Up-to-date Picture Theatre in North Wales.

Telephone - - Bangor 59

Sole Proprietor and Licencee J. R. SARONIE. | Resident Manager A. E. ALLBRIGHT.

*Mr. Saronie first centered his business activities on the Mersey side as a Professional Portrait Photographer, with Branches extending over England, Scotland and Wales. Early in 1906 he visualised the present entertainment of the people, and to-day he is looked upon as one of the most progressive Pioneers in the Kinematograph World.*

**FIRST IN 1896** ★ **FOREMOST IN 1934**

Into the life and interests of Bangor has come a new power of entertainment — THE PLAZA THEATRE and SUPER CINEMA — dedicated to your happiness.

THIS Afternoon's socially brilliant gathering see a Theatre in keeping with Bangor's importance and progress—a theatre of charm and beauty—a theatre with a scale of entertainment unparalleled not only in the history of Bangor, but in that of the whole of Caernarvonshire. :: :: :: :: ::

**NEW** Delights await you on the "Plaza" screen. Standards of Talking Picture Production. High Fidelity recording, reproducing the human voice and music with life-like realism.

*Truly a New Era in Entertainment has begun*

*In my early teens, I used to go every week to the Plaza, or City or County Theatre in Bangor. Three completely different picture houses, the poshest being the Plaza. We bought a ticket for one shilling and between two houses sneaked to the 1/9d seats. Later on we bought tickets at 1/9d and sneaked to the 2/4d seats. The double seats were at the back of the 2/4d and also upstairs - back few rows only of the 2/7d. When we were treated to the pictures by a boy - it was to the 2/7d. I remember one - my friend and I were taken to the 2/7d by two country lads from the heart of Anglesey. One film was by Jacques Cousteau with some wonderful scenery in colour. These two lads were so engrossed in the film, my friend and I got up and left. They never missed us!*

**Eira Lloyd Crocombe, Bangor, Gwynedd.**

Isod: yr Arcadia, Bangor, cyn ei dymchwel er mwyn adeiladu sinema newydd foethus y Plaza yn 1934 (gweler dalen o'r rhaglen agoriadol ar y dde).

*Below: the Arcadia Cinema, Bangor, before its demolition in order to build Saronie's luxury Plaza Cinema in 1934 (see the extract from the opening programme on the right).*

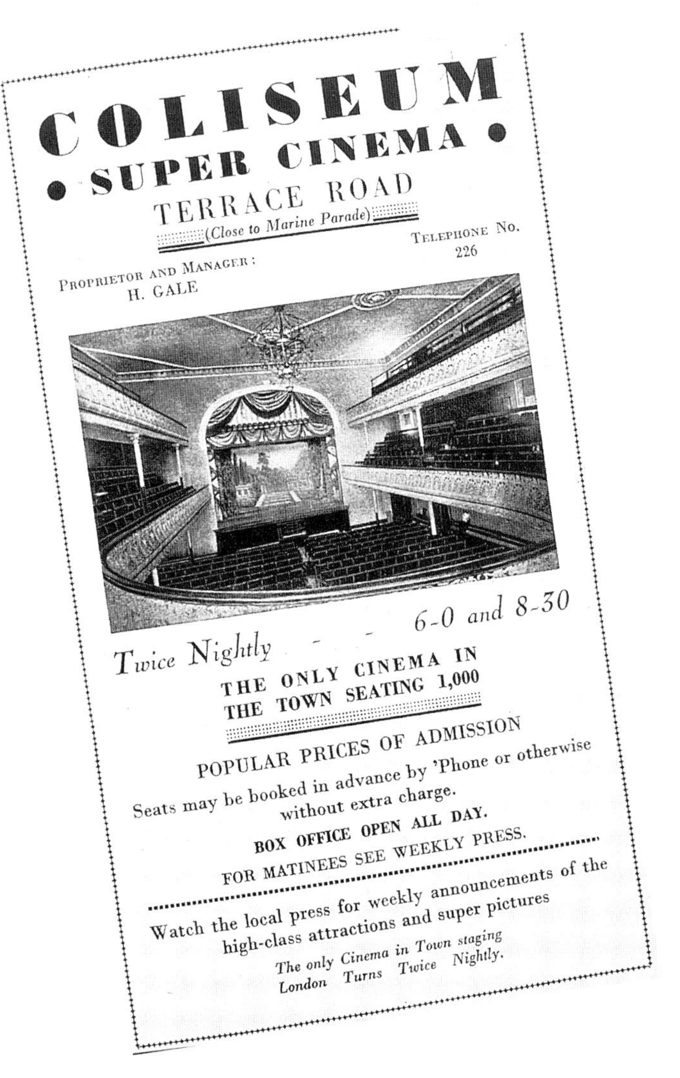
COLISEUM
SUPER CINEMA
TERRACE ROAD
(Close to Marine Parade)
TELEPHONE No. 226
PROPRIETOR AND MANAGER: H. GALE
Twice Nightly - - - 6-0 and 8-30
THE ONLY CINEMA IN THE TOWN SEATING 1,000
POPULAR PRICES OF ADMISSION
Seats may be booked in advance by 'Phone or otherwise without extra charge.
BOX OFFICE OPEN ALL DAY.
FOR MATINEES SEE WEEKLY PRESS.
Watch the local press for weekly announcements of the high-class attractions and super pictures
The only Cinema in Town staging London Turns Twice Nightly.

*Going to the pictures in the Pier Pavilion was a unique experience because when you sat in your comfortable plush seat, you could hear the sea slapping against the wall of the Promenade fifty yards behind you. On really stormy nights, when big waves crashed into the stanchions on which the building stood, the whole fabric shook, and when we walked back down the Pier from the cinema entrance, spray and sea water leapt up through the gaps between the boards making our shoes wet and salty. Inside, the cinema was comfortable, with no obstructions, large green plush seats and lots of legroom... The Coliseum, on the other hand, stood in Terrace Road; it had been a Theatre and Music Hall in its heyday, and my mother had a photograph of herself on stage in a mammoth production of 'Goldilocks and the Three Bears' which had been performed by local schools in 1912. By the thirties the old theatre was rather shabby; in fact some of the seats were missing altogether, and anyone coming in late, feeling their way in the dark, made sure there was something to sit on before they sat! There were stalls and an upper and lower circle. The upper circle, affectionately known as 'The Gods' didn't have seats; just a bench which ran around the horse shoe shape of the circle and if you sat up there, for the pricely sum of one shilling you got a nasty crick in your neck from trying to see the whole of the screen.*

**Mrs Beryl Ellis, ganed / born Aberystwyth, Ceredigion**

Adeilad sinc oedd Sinema'r Parc... Cofiaf un brawd yn eistedd yn un o'r seddau ffrynt ac yn rhyw led awgrymu ei fod wedi llwyddo i gyfrif blew oedd ar fron yr arwr y noson honno mewn ffilm am y Gorllewin Gwyllt. Ys gwn i ai yn y sinema hon eisteddodd Groucho Marx pan y cyfeiriodd am ffilm De Mille *Samson and Delilah*: dyma'r ffilm lle mae bronnau Samson yn fwy na rhai Delilah!? Gan mai adeilad sinc oedd Sinema'r Parc cyfeiriodd un boi galluog ei fod yn mynd i mewn yn aml heb docyn drwy gymorth teclyn agor tun! Diffygion sinema sinc oedd ei bod yn agored i'r tywydd. Hynny yw, glaw yn curo ar y to, a phoethder y lle fel popty. Bûm yno ar y ddau achlysur hwn. Un tro roedd y ffilm seiliedig ar fywyd yn yr India yn cael ei dangos - *The Rain's Came* (1939). Tua'r diwedd daeth y glaw a'r daeargryn yn y stori, ond yr un pryd roedd yn amhosibl clywed y sain gan y glaw yn curo yn ddi-dor ar do y sinema. Dyma yn wir beth oedd sain 'stereo' ymhell cyn i unrhyw sinema arall fynd i gostau mawr i osod y taclau i greu y fath awyrgylch! Buaswn yn bersonol yn awgrymu i'r Park Cinema ddangos

Sinema'r Parc, Blaenau Ffestiniog, cyn ei dymchwel.
*The Park Cinema, Blaenau Ffestiniog, past its heyday.*

dim ond ffilmiau lle mae glaw trwm ynddynt, a brolio'r ymgais fel SAIN YN DOD O BOBMAN YN HOLLOL FEL O DDIFRIF! Tro arall cofiaf yn dda fynd i'r Parc i weld y ffilm *Beau Geste* (1939 eto - blwyddyn dda i'r sinema hon greu awyrgylch!) Nefoedd! Cofiaf un olygfa lle roedd y gwron yn llusgo drwy'r tywod tanllyd am lymaid o ddŵr oedd ddim yn bod. Roedd hi yng nghanol Awst poeth pan ddangoswyd y ffilm hon, a'r adeilad sinc yn gwegian gan y gwres. Ond cofiwch, fe wnaeth gwerthwyr yr hufen iâ ffortiwn yn ystod yr ysbaid!

*The Park Cinema was a zinc building, but if I remember rightly, it had a wide screen... I remember one chap sitting in the front seats who suggested that he had succeeded in counting all the hairs on the hero's chest that night in a film about the Wild West. I wonder if it was in this cinema that Groucho Marx remarked about De Mille's film* Samson and Delilah*: 'This is the film where Samson's chest was bigger than Delilah's'? As the Park Cinema was in a zinc building, one clever chap said that he could get in frequently without paying with the help of a tin opener! The disadvantage of a zinc cinema was that it was at the mercy of the weather - that is, the rain banging on the roof, and the hot weather turning the place into an oven. I was there on two such occasions. On the first, they were showing a film about life in India called* The Rains Came *(1939). Towards the end, the rains and earthquake came in the story, but at the same time you could hardly hear the sound because of the rain thundering down on the cinema roof. This truly was stereo sound, before any other cinema went to the great expense to install equipment to create such an atmosphere... Another time, I remember going to the Park to see the film* Beau Geste *(1939 again - a good year for creating an atmosphere in this cinema!) Heavens! I remember one scene where the hero was dragging himself through the burning desert looking for water that didn't exist. This film was shown in the middle of a very hot August, and the zinc building was sagging in the heat. But the ice cream vendors made a fortune in the interval!*

**Emyr Owen, Blaenau Ffestiniog, Gwynedd**

Lle bwyta a lolfa Sinema'r Plaza, Abertawe, tua 1931.
*The café and lounge of the Plaza Cinema, Swansea, c. 1931.*

*You went in to the Regal - there were three large doors, two on the side and a double one in the centre. When the people came out they opened the three doors. When you went in only the centre doors were open. And you had the lady in the box - she was a big stout lady, and she used to have her hair marcel waved, you know. You went in and there weren't any sides, only the centre seating inside, and they had this big wooden partition up the top [that] you could lean on and look at the films if you were grown up, but the children couldn't see over it. Upstairs then they had two aisles going down, the centre bit, and the two side sections. In the late 1930s they had it all done out, and they had plush seats. The plush was about six inches thick and they had double seats for the courting couples... I used to go to the Plaza [in Swansea]. Very posh it was, going to the Plaza. I don't know why they got rid of that and put the Odeon there, because it was a lovely building, the Plaza. Upstairs in the Plaza you had a coffee shop. It had very large windows and you had the tables and chairs where you could have coffee and look. Basket chairs, you know. You could look out on the main road and people passing. It was really lovely there.*

**Mrs Eirona Richards, Treforys, Abertawe / Morriston, Swansea, ganed / born 1928**

Rwy'n credu mai swllt oedd y pris safonol am fynediad o'i gymharu â swllt a naw i'r Empire, a dau swllt a thair i orial y Majestic lle yr oedd rhywun yn teimlo fel pe bai wedi cael teyrnas. Roedd yno le hefyd a elwid y *cafe lounge*, ac os yr oeddech chi wedi cael eich gweld yn y fan honno roeddech chi'n werth eich meithrin. Un llawr oedd yn yr Empire. Lle digon glanwaith a threfnus ond yn chwanog i ddangos rhyw ffilmiau ar led ymyl, ffilmiau arswyd y cyfnod fuasai ddim yn codi ofn ar iâr a chywion heddiw: Karloff a Bela Lugosi a'r criw Ffrancynsteinaidd rheiny. Roedd y sefydliad yn hysbysebu drwy osod lluniau ar waliau'r Pendis, y tu ôl i wydrau. Byr fuasai oes rheiny heddiw! Wrth gwrs erbyn fy amser i roedd y *talkies* wedi cyrraedd, er fod y Guild Hall yn dal i ddangos lluniau mud Buster Keaton a' r Keystone Cops i lenwi bylchau. Sŵn piano oedd y cyfeiliant er nad oedd yr offeryn yn weladwy fel yn y dyddiau cynnar. Roedd yna neuadd luniau fechan yn Llanberis hefyd: y Luxor yn cael ei chadw gan Mrs. Waleham. Roedd y fynedfa wrth ochr y sgrîn i wynebu'r bobl. Rhyw naw ceiniog oedd y pris i gael eistedd yn y man a fynnoch; yr hwyrddyfodiaid yn gorfod eistedd yng ngwyneb y sgrîn i ddatblygu cric gwegil a chael eu byddaru. Gwelid rhai yn gwyro neu blygu i'r ochr i osgoi cael eu mathru gan drên neu ruthr gwŷr meirch a ddeuai yn syth amdanynt. Roedd y cariadon yn ymryson am y seddau cefn, a 'doedd diben gofyn iddynt hwy ai da neu gwael oedd y ffilm.

**John E. Williams, Llanrug, Gwynedd yn disgrifio sinemâu Caernarfon a Llanberis**

Tu fewn i'r Picture House, y Stryd Fawr, Abertawe, tua 1930. Agorwyd y sinema hon yn 1915, ond fe'i dinistriwyd yn ystod y bomio ym mis Rhagfyr, 1941.

*The auditorium of the Picture House, High Street, Swansea. This cinema was built in 1915, but destroyed in the Blitz of December 1941.*

Lolfa a lle bwyta'r Picture House, Abertawe, tua 1930.

*The café and lounge of the Picture House, Swansea, c.1930.*

*I think the standard entrance price was a shilling, compared with 1/9d to go to the Empire, and 2/3d to sit in the gallery of the Majestic, where you would feel like a lord. There was also a café lounge there, and if you were seen there it was worth making your acquaintance. The Empire was a single storey building. It was clean and orderly enough, but it tended to show marginal films, horror films that wouldn't raise a hair nowadays - Karloff and Bela Lugosi and that Frankenstinian crew. The establishment would advertise by placing photos on the wall, behind glass. Those wouldn't last long nowadays! Of course, by my time, the talkies had arrived, although the Guild Hall continued to show Buster Keaton and the Keystone Cops to fill in the gaps. It was piano accompaniment, although the instrument wasn't visible as in the early days. There was a small picture house in Llanberis too: the Luxor kept by Mrs Waleham. The entrance was next to the screen facing the audience. It used to cost about ninepence to sit where you wanted; the latecomers had to sit facing the screen to develop a crick in their necks and be deafened. Some were seen ducking or moving aside to avoid being run over by a train or cavalry coming straight at them. The courting couples would fight for the back seats, and it was no use asking them how good or bad the film was.*

**John E. Williams, Llanrug, Gwynedd describing the cinemas of Caernarfon and Llanberis**

*We went to the Castle cinema to see a film and on the second landing there was a tearoom. I'll never forget the smell of the coffee there. There were all wicker chairs and beautiful big rooms, and the bar with the coffee machine. You could have tea, coffee and cakes, and my birthday party or birthday treat was to go there with my grandmother, sit and have coffee and then go and see the film.*

**Vincent Thomas, Merthyr Tudful, ganed / born 1927**

*I've got to tell you all about the Castle Cinema. That was my favourite place because it was - what we said - posh. First of all they had seats that were red plush. All the ceilings were outlined in gilt and they had a chandelier above all things and a beautiful stage with lovely big red drapes on it.*

*And they had the organ, the electric organ, and the man that played the organ was called Gene Lyn. He was a little man and one thing I remember about him, he always wore a white suit or a black evening suit, and either a red carnation or a white gardenia. He was very, very with-it as far as dress goes those days. When the film started he would come up from the pits, and as the organ was rising up he'd be bowing on either side, royalty, to everybody in the theatre. And then the lights would change. They had wonderful spotlights, and he appeared to be lavender, the organ and him, then a pale blue. It was absolutely wonderful to watch him. Then, perhaps half way through this, there'd be a big sign that would be flashed across: 'Trip to Blackpool run by the Castle Cinema' and then he'd be playing music like 'Oh I do want to be beside the Seaside', everything to fit in with it.*

**Mrs Iris Roderick Thomas, Merthyr Tudful, ganed/born 1927**

Idris Thomas, organydd sinema'r Empire, Caerdydd, o 1936 tan 1947. Tynnwyd yr organ o'r sinema yn 1955 a'i werthu i eglwys ym Mryste.

*Idris Thomas, the organist at the Empire Cinema, Cardiff, from 1936 to 1947. The organ was removed in 1955 and sold to a church in Bristol.*

Y sinema yn Neuadd Ogwen, Bethesda, Gwynedd.
*Cinema interior, Neuadd Ogwen, Bethesda, Gwynedd.*

*Both the Celtic and the Conway were owned and run by Mr. D.M Davies and each cinema had its own individual programme of films... . The larger of the two and the most popular in Aberystwyth was the Celtic... . This was a single level cinema reputed to have formerly been a swimming pool. It was notorious for its sloping floor, a favourite trick being to roll empty pop bottles down the aisles from the back rows. These bottles expertly placed would gather momentum creating a tremendous roar on the concrete uncarpeted floor before colliding with the stage at the front and disintegrating to mixed roars of approval and disapproval from the audience! It was the Celtic that I saw many of the more memorable films of the time including all the James Bond and Clint Eastwood pictures,* Lawrence of Arabia, Woodstock, Women in Love, The Devils of London, *etc. In those days cinema were really DARK and not semi-illuminated by safety or other lights as they are today. Smoking was rife and although there may have been some No Smoking signs, these were blatantly ignored. Heating was usually by dubious-looking, wall-mounted gas or electric heaters which gave off a smoky glow and occasionally and alarmingly spouted flames. Through this dark, smoky and spluttering atmosphere cut the searchlight beam of the projector and a backward glance over your shoulder would reveal the face of the projectionist peering our from his porthole like a machinegunner in his pillbox.*
**David Subacchi, Aberystwyth, Ceredigion, ganed / born 1955**

*If you went in the balcony - well, that was showing off. That was something else. We never went to the balcony, but there were areas that were ours. They were marked out. There was a culture about it... You sort of started in the front row as kids, where you made a lot of row and you were told off and all the rest of it. You started at the front row and you worked your way back as you matured... Our group in the youth club, we had the bottom row at the bottom of the steps, and then later on, as you were courting, you were in the back row at the top of the steps. But that's the progression that you made. Part of the culture. And it was great fun.*
**Tom Davies, Oakdale, Caerffili, ganed / born 1932**

Sinema Institiwt y Gweithwyr, Oakdale, a godwyd yn 1927.
*The New Hall or 'Picture House' at Oakdale Workmen's Institute, built 1927.*

# Y 'Cosi' Sinema
## *The Laugh and Scratch*

Mae llu o atgofion yn ffrwydro i'r wyneb, atgofion am yr Empire. Roedd yma filoedd o ymwelwyr bychan, bychan yn y *flea pit* hwn. Un tro, gwnaeth y papur lleol gamgymeriad (anfwriadol gobeithio) a chyfeirio yn y broliant at y sinema hwn fel y 'Cosi Cinema' yn hytrach na'r 'Cosy Cinema'! Dywedir yn llên gwerin Stiniog fod brawd wedi disgyn i gysgu yn y sedd gefn ac wedi deffro yn un o'r seddau blaen, ond cario dychymyg yn rhy bell yw hyn!

*A number of memories explode in my mind, memories of the Empire. There were thousands of very small visitors in this flea pit. Once upon a time, the local newspaper made a mistake (hopefully unintentional) and advertised this cinema as the 'Cosi Cinema'* [cosi *is the Welsh word for itching*] *instead of the 'Cosy Cinema'. According to the folklore of Blaenau Ffestiniog, one chap fell asleep in the back seats and woke up in one of the front seats, but that's carrying imagination too far!*

**Emyr Owen, Blaenau Ffestiniog, Gwynedd**

Gadael Sinema'r Empire, Blaenau Ffestiniog, ar ôl bod yn gwylio un o ffilmiau Charlie Chaplin, tua 1930.
*Leaving the Empire Cinema, Blaenau Ffestiniog, after seeing a Charlie Chaplin film, c.1930.*

# Y 'Cosi' Sinema
## *The Laugh and Scratch*

Roedd yna dair sinema yng Nghaernarfon: y Guild Hall, yr Empire, ac yn ddiweddarach y Majestic - y ddwy olaf wedi eu hadeiladau i'r pwrpas a'r Guild Hall wedi'i haddasu o hen neuadd. Serch hynny roedd yno oriel, ac ar brydiau adloniant ychwanegol i wylio'r ffilmiau, ac yr oedd rhai yn mynd mor bell â dweud fod yno chwain, ac yn dangos eu gwrymiau i brofi eu haeriaedau.

*There were three cinemas in Caernarfon: the Guild Hall, the Empire and later the Majestic. The last two were purpose-built, and the Guild Hall had been adapted from an old hall. Despite that, it had a gallery and on some occasions additional entertainment to watching the films. Some went as far as to say that there were fleas there, and would show their weals to prove their accusations.*

**John E. Williams, Llanrug, Gwynedd**

Un peth arbennig oedd ynghylch Pictiwrs Bach Llanberis: yr oedd chwarel Dinorwic yn ei hanterth yr adeg hynny cyn y rhyfel, a hogia sir Fôn yn dod yno i weithio ac yn aros yn y Barics o ddydd Llun hyd deuddeg dydd Sadwrn. Bechgyn ieuainc o bedair ar ddeg i fyny ac yn dod i'r pictiwrs yn enwedig i weld y *serials*. Yr oedd sôn am chwain yn y Barics, ac yn naturiol yr oedd yr hogia yn cario y chwain ar eu cyrff, ac yr oedd seddau wedi eu neilltuo ar eu cyfer. Nid oedd neb am eistedd yn agos atynt rhag ofn codi whanen, yr hogia yn llygadu'r merched a'r merched yr hogia, ond yn cadw yn ddigon pell a llawer o hwyl ynghylch hynny. Yr oedd yna ddywediad nad oedd dim pwysa gwaed ar ddynion y Barics am fod y chwain yn eu sugno. *'No high blood pressure'*. Yn y diwedd mi aeth cariad yn drech na'r chwain ac amryw wedi priodi a byw yn y pentrefi cyfagos.

*One particular thing about the Pictures at Llanberis: Dinorwic quarry was in its heyday then, before the war, and Anglesey lads would come there to work, staying in the Barracks from Monday till mid-day on Saturday. They were young boys aged fourteen and upwards, and they'd come to the pictures especially to see the serials. There was talk of fleas in the Barracks, and naturally the boys carried the fleas on their persons. Seats were set aside for them, and no-one wanted to sit next to them in case they picked up a flea. The lads would eye the girls and the girls the lads, but would keep far enough away and there'd be a lot of fun regarding that. There was a saying that the Barracks men did not suffer from high blood pressure because the fleas sucked their blood. In the end, love was stronger than the fleas, and many of them married and came to live in the neighbouring villages.*

**Hugh R. Jones, Llanberis, Gwynedd**

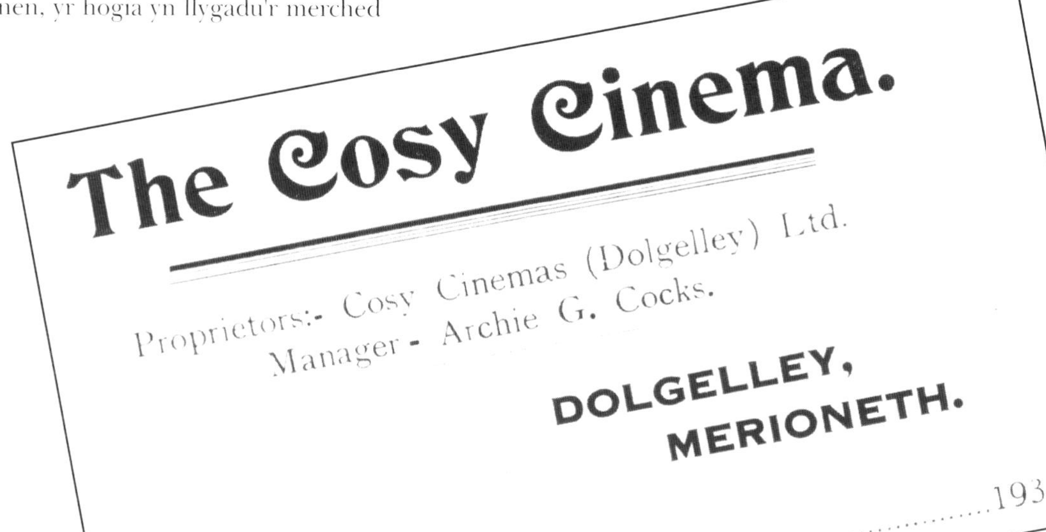

# Y 'Cosi' Sinema
## *The Laugh and Scratch*

*We were very fortunate really in Merthyr, because we had three cinemas and two live shows. So number one preference was the Castle because it was posh, you know. Then we had the Palace which showed normally Columbia films, and then we had the Electric which we called the Bughouse, because you never came back from the Bughouse without having some livestock on you. But that was the first cinema in Merthyr and the first film they showed, before my time, was* The Charge of the Light Brigade. *I've got a photograph somewhere that I must let you have - it shows you the very night that they opened the Electric Cinema and all the dignitaries sitting outside. It was a great place... They had benches in the front where all the children sat, and when the cowboys came on, they'd all stand on the seats and they'd be screaming 'Give it to him!' and this and that and the other. Then if something came on that was quite romantic, they'd be shouting 'Ah! Put it off! Sloppy stuff!' Then they'd be sitting down having their sandwiches or whatever they brought with them... My mother used to say 'Now don't go to the Electric, you mustn't go to the Electric,' because as soon as I got home I'd have to strip and she'd search me - put me in the bath, you know, with the tub in front of the fire, to make sure I had nothing on me.*

**Mrs Iris Roderick Thomas, Merthyr Tudful, ganed / born 1927**

Agoriad yr Electric Theatre, Merthyr Tudful, 1920au.
*The opening of the Electric Theatre, Merthyr Tydfil, 1920s.*

*The Pontlottyn cinema was called the Fleapit locally, so I realise now it was a fire hazard. It was longish and narrow, divided crosswise by two steps so that the third was higher than the other two. One entered along a slight slope between the outside wall and a wooden partition the length of the top third, turning behind the partition to the gangway for the upper seats. The rows extended to the opposite wall and could not have been more than twelve seats in length. I remember it vividly because on the last occasion we went, there was a fire. My cousin, grandfather and I were sitting near the front of the top section and became aware of an odd smell. Grandfather realised that a man in front, who had been smoking fairly continuously, had dropped a cigarette end which had smouldered on the wooden flooring and I think woollen gloves on the floor. Unfortunately when told quietly about the incipient fire, instead of listening to grandfather's suggestion, the smoker leapt to his feet shouting 'Fire, fire!' The resultant chaos was frightful, adults and children rushing for the exit down the gangway slope or for an exit through toilets at the bottom of the gangway near the screen. I think we moved back out of the way whilst my grandfather and acquaintance of his, who had been sitting behind, used their feet and coats to try to put out or at least prevent the fire from spreading. Eventually someone brought buckets to throw on the floor. I can remember seeing the sparks and tiny flames running along more and more floor boards and the smouldering smell of the seats. Fortunately there were few real injuries - probably not many people there and the chaos magnified by a child's eye. The cinema was, I think, closed a few months later.*

**Mrs Irene Thomas yn sôn am sinema Pontlotyn, Caerffili.**

**Mrs Irene Thomas describing the cinema at Pontlottyn, Caerphilly.**

CINEMAS

PARK HALL.
Sydney Greenstreet, Peter Lorre
in Eric Ambler's Terrific Mystery Thriller
"THE MASK OF DIMITRIOS"
Showing at 2.25, 5.25, 8.25.
WILL HAY
'The GHOST of ST. MICHAEL'S'
Showing at 1.0, 4.0, 7.0.

EMPIRE, Gaumont-British.
MURDER WITH MUSIC!
LAIRD GEORGE LINDA
CREGAR SANDERS DARNELL
"HANGOVER SQUARE"
"A" DAILY 2.25 5.30 8.35.
Martha O'DRISCOLL Noah BEERY, Jn.
in "PASS TO ROMANCE"
"U" DAILY 1.5 4.10 7.15.
Soon: "A SONG TO REMEMBER."

CAPITOL, Cardiff. Tel. 6477-8.
ALAN LADD
LORETTA YOUNG
with SUSAN HAYWARD in
"AND NOW TO-MORROW"
At 12.15, 3.0, 5.45, 8.25. (A)
GLORIA JEAN, KIRBY GRANT
"I'LL REMEMBER APRIL"
Showing at 1.45, 4.30, 7.15. (A)

OLYMPIA, CARDIFF. A.B.C. Theatre.
GREER GARSON
WALTER PIDGEON
Edward ARNOLD, Agnes MOORHEAD
"MRS. PARKINGTON"
At 2.0, 4.50, 7.40. (A)
"ANIMAL WONDERLAND"
A Picture That is Different.
Showing at 1.15, 4.0, 7.0. (U)

ODEON, CARDIFF.
2 GIANT PICTURES ON SAME BILL
MERLE FRANCHOT
OBERON TONE
"DARK WATERS"
At 1.45, 5.0, 8.15. (A)
CHARLES JEAN
BOYER ARTHUR
'HISTORY IS MADE AT NIGHT'
At 12.5, 3.20, 6.35. (A)

QUEENS, CARDIFF. A.B.C. Theatre.
ROY ROGERS
King of the Cowboys,
and TRIGGER in
"YELLOW ROSE OF TEXAS"
with DALE EVANS, BOB NOLAN
At 1.30, 3.45, 6.0, 8.20. (U)
STEPHANIE BACHELOR
'The PORT of FORTY THIEVES'
At 2.45, 5.0, 7.20. (A)

PAVILION CARDIFF
Don AMECHE Joan BENNETT
"GIRL TROUBLE"
AT 2.40 5.40 8.40
ELLERY QUEEN in
"THE MURDER RING"
AT 1.20 4.0 7.0
SONGS, THE ORGAN, AND YOU.
At 5.25 and 8.25.
The Programme of the Week—Every Week!

GLOBE, Penylan.
JOEL McCREA, BETTY FIELD
"THE GREAT MOMENT"
Ray Milland, Patricia Morison
"UNTAMED" (Technicolour).
Continuous from 5.0. Sat. 2.0.

COLISEUM, Canton.
RANDOLPH SCOTT, ALAN CURTIS
"GUNG HO"
Also "ROSE OF TRALEE"
Continuous from 5.0. Sat. 2.0.

RIALTO, Whitchurch.
PAULETTE GODDARD, SONNY TUFTS
"I LOVE A SOLDIER"
Also "RAIDERS OF SAN JOAQUIN"
Continuous from 5.30. Sat. 4.0.

AVENUE CINEMA DE LUXE,
Richard Dix and [illegible] in
WHISTLER (A.) ([illegible], 8.55)
Rogers and Mary Lee in THE COWBO
THE SENORITA (U.) (1.55, 4.40,
News. We open at 4 o'clock Thursd
1.30 Friday and Saturday.

COUNTY SUPER CINEMA, Ru
Laurence Olivier, Penelope Ward in
DEMI-PARADISE (U.) (6.0, 8.10
1.50). Richard Arlen, Jean Park
ALASKA HIGHWAY (U.) (3.40,
News 4.50, 8.0.

CANTON SUPER CINEMA (C
of Library-st.).—Olivia De Havilland
Sonny Tufts in GOVERNMENT GIR
(3.0, 5.45, 8.30). Ruth Terry and
Livingston in GOOD-NIGHT, SW
HEART (U.) (1.55, 4.40, 7.25
Continuous. Thurs. and Sat. 1.30, Fri.

GAIETY, CITY-ROAD.
Abbott and Costello in LOST IN A H
(A) (at 5.40, 8.30). Jerome Cowa
Faye Emerson in FIND THE B
MAILER (A) (at 4.35, 7.25). "[illegible]
Time" and News. Doors Open Tu-da
Sat. 1.30.

MONICO, Rhiwbina (Tel. Whit.
Phyllis Calvert and Stewart Gran
MADONNA OF THE SEVEN MOO
(2.30, 5.15, 8.5). Richard Travis a
Bishop in ESCAPE FROM CRIM
(1.40, 4.25, 7.15). Open Thurs. an
1.30, Fri. 4.0.

NINIAN CINEMA, Penarth-ro
Stewart Granger and Phyllis Calve
MADONNA OF THE SEVEN MOONS
5.5, 8.10). Judy Canova in LOUIS
HAYRIDE (at 1.50, 6.55). Doors ope
Thursday and Saturday; 3.30 Frida

PLAZA, NORTH-ROAD.
Fred MacMurray and Paulette Go
THE FOREST RANGERS (A.) (3.0
8.30), in Technicolour. CALL OF
SOUTH SEAS (A.), Janet Martin and
Lane (2.0, 4.45, 7.30). Open Thur
Sat. 1.30, Fri., 4 p.m.

REGENT SUPER CINEMA, E
Phyllis Calvert and Stewart Gran
MADONNA OF THE SEVEN MOON
(at 2.0, 5.5, and 8.10). Michael Am
Julie Bishop in I WAS FRAMED (A
3.55 and 7.0). Open Thurs. and S
1.30 p.m.; Fri., 3.30 p.m.

SPLOTT SUPER CINEMA.
George Formby and Robertson Hare,
SNOOPS TO CONQUER (U.) (2.30,
8.15). Roger Pryor and Eve Arden,
COULDN'T SAY NO (U.) (1.30,
7.15). Open Thurs., Sat., 1.15; F

TIVOLI, LLANDAFF.
Thurs., Fri., at 4 p.m.; Sat., 2.0.
De Havilland, Sonny Tufts in GOV
MENT GIRL (U.) (5.13, 8.16) (Sat.,
Ruth Terry, Robt. Livingston, GOOD N
SWEETHEART (U.). News. (5.3, 8.6)
2.0). Interest.

WASHINGTON PENA
OLIVIA DE HAVILLAND, SONNY T
"GOVERNMENT GIRL
At 2.55, 5.45, 8.30. (U)
ROBERT LIVINGSTON, RUTH TE
"GOODNIGHT SWEETHEA
At 1.45, 4.35, 7.25. (U)
NEWS 4.25, 7.15. INTER

WINDSOR PENA
Fred MACMURRAY, Paulette GOD
"THE FOREST RANGER
At 3.5, 5.50, 9.35. (A)
BRAD TAYLOR, RUTH TERR
"SING NEIGHBOUR, SIN
At 1.45, 4.30, 7.15. (U)
INTEREST NEWS.

Y dewis a wynebai trigolion ardal Caerdydd, 1940au!

*The choice facing Cardiff cinemagoers, 1940s!*

# Commissionaires, Usherettes

*The usherettes of course, we knew them all and they were all smart girls. They were all in their uniforms, red uniforms with gold down their skirts, pill box hat. They thought they were the business, of course! They'd run the cinema - they knew all  the bad ones coming in and they knew all the good ones. I was fortunate because I always gave them some sweets or a few chocolates or something like that, you see, and they always put me in some good seats. We got on great, but they were strict as well. If there was any real nonsense, they would come with the torch and say 'Come on, out! I've warned you before!' And out you'd have to go.  And if you didn't go, they'd get the manager and they'd put the lights up, stop the film to get you out. But I was never as bad as that.*

**Vincent Thomas, Merthyr Tudful, ganed / born 1927**

*He was the dogsbody, he did every single thing. He inserted the photographs in the front windows, 'cause those days when you had a very important film - you know an 'A' film - they'd have all the black and white photographs to put in the window, different scenes, and he'd be there. Then he'd be pasting the posters on the board, which were massive, outside. He'd be the commissionaire. He'd be comforting children if there was a film and they started to cry. He'd go and comfort them, take them in for some ice-cream.*

**Mrs Iris Roderick Thomas, Merthyr Tudful, ganed / born 1927**

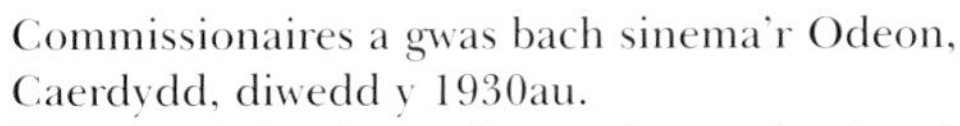

Commissionaires a gwas bach sinema'r Odeon, Caerdydd, diwedd y 1930au.
*Two commissionaires and a pageboy employed at the Odeon Cinema, Cardiff, late 1930s.*

# Commissionaires, Usherettes

*[The Coliseum] was built on the upper floors of a block of shops, and to get to the box office, you had to climb a flight of steep stone steps. At the foot of these, resplendent in a pale blue uniform with lots of medals on his chest, stood Dai Jones the Commissionaire, shouting 'Seats in the Two and Threepennys! Main feature starts in few minutes!' And at the top of the steps, waiting like a little fat spider to entice you into her web, sat Mrs Gale the Proprietress, ensconced behind a tiny window by the ticket machine. Only about five feet tall, and about the same in circumference, she always wore black, with a shawl around her shoulders, and a Spanish comb in her chignon. She had tiny feet, and eyes like jet beads.*

**Mrs Beryl Ellis, ganed / born Aberystwyth, Ceredigion.**

Mrs Davies oedd yn cadw'r lle heb fawr gynorthwy heblaw dyn y lantern. Hi oedd gofalwr y drws a'r hogan dicedi ac ar brydiau yr *usherette* hufen rew, ac yn cael ei galw yn gyfrifol gan yr holl gynulleidfa pan fyddai pethau yn mynd yn groes, fel ffilm yn torri, llenni'r sgrîn yn gwrthod agor, y golau neu'r swn yn pallu, pan fyddai pawb yn creu ei ddeialog ei hun ar dop ei lais. Roedd ganddi lond ei dwylo, yr hen Fusus, a fyddai hi ddim yn brin o'u defnyddio nhw ar y rhai anystywallt.

*Mrs Davies looked after the place without much help, apart from the projectionist. She was the doorkeeper, the ticket girl, and sometimes the ice cream usherette, and was called to account whenever anything went wrong, such as the film breaking, the curtains refusing to open, or when the light or the sound would not work, and everyone would create their own dialogue at the tops of their voices. She had her hands full, the old Mrs, and she wasn't averse to using them on the unruly.*

**John E. Williams, Llanrug, Gwynedd**

Staff y Coliseum, Aberystwyth, yn cymryd rhan mewn ymgyrch gyhoeddusrwydd ar gyfer *The King Steps Out*, Medi 1936. Enillodd Mrs Gale, rheolwraig y sinema (yr ail o'r chwith), wobr am yr ymgyrch gan Columbia Pictures.
*The staff of the Coliseum Cinema, Aberystwyth, taking part in a publicity stunt for The King Steps Out, September 1936. Mrs Gale, the cinema's manageress (2nd from left), won an award for the publicity for this film from Columbia Pictures.*

# Commissionaires, Usherettes

*The usherettes, flashing their torches about in the dark, wore black dresses and little white aprons like the maids in French farces, and the Manager, Mr Daniels, a tall elegant ex-soldier, did his rounds in evening dress, complete with dinner jacket, gleaming white shirt and bow tie. Woe betide any children misbehaving in the 'ninepennies' in the front when he walked down the aisle during the interval between the second feature and the 'big picture'.*

**Mrs Beryl Ellis yn sôn am y Pier Cinema yn Aberystwyth, Ceredigion**
**Mrs Beryl Ellis describing the Pier Cinema, Aberystwyth, Ceredigion.**

Odd *Hall* y Cwm wedi'ny lawer fwy o le... *Workmen's Hall*, 'na beth odd yr enw cywir arno fe. A'r *workmen* odd yn redeg e, chwel. Dodi *manager* miwn, ond odd pwyllgor 'da nw wedi'ny yn redeg e. A'dd dim *usherettes* - y dinon odd yn neud gwaith yr *usherettes* os odd ishe. On ni gyd â ofan y *manager*. Pan odd e'n dod rown, odd pobun yn dawel. Och chi ddim stampo'ch trâd pry'ny cofiwch! Ond gwetwch chi bod bachgen yn dodi 'i law rown sgwydde y ferch odd e'n garu - '*Out! Unseemly behaviour!*' weten nw. Weles i mewn blynydde wedi'ny fel odd pethe'n y Globe yn Clydach - wel on i'n meddwl bo fi yn Sodom a Gomorrah, gweud y gwir 'thoch chi, i gym'aru â *Hall* y Cwm, ife. Odd y gwr yn gweu'tho'i pwy ddwyrnod, 'Ti'n cofio yn *Hall* y Cwm? Fentret ti ddim dodi dy fraich rown merch achos bydde fe'n towlu ti mâs!'

*Cwm Hall was a much larger place... Workmen's Hall, that was its correct name. It was the workmen that ran it, you see. They put a manager in, but they had a committee to run it. And there were no usherettes - the men would do the work of usherettes if it was needed. We were all afraid of the manager. When he came around, everyone was quiet. You didn't stamp your feet then, mind! But say a boy put his arm round his sweetheart's shoulders - 'Out! Unseemly behaviour!' they'd say. I saw years later how things were in the Globe in Clydach - well, I thought I was in Sodom and Gomorrah, to tell you the truth, compared with Cwm Hall. My husband was telling me the other night, 'Do you remember Cwm Hall? You wouldn't dare put your arm round a girl because he'd throw you out!'*

**Mrs Peggy Jones, Brynaman, Sir Gaerfyrddin / Carmarthen shire, ganed / born 1921.**

Y sêr cyfredol oedd William S Hart, Lon Chaney a Chaplin, Paulette Goddard a Mae West, Laurel *and* Hardy, wrth gwrs, ac yn ddiweddarach, Garbo a Gable. Roedd Don Ameche hefyd yn boblogaidd, Barrymore, a Wallace Beery a oedd yn dibynnu mwy ar ei bersonoliaeth na'i dalent. Byddai mewn ffilmiau am y Bowery a'r Gorllewin, ac unwaith fo oedd Pancho Villa. Fy nihyryn hoff i oedd Beery. Fy ffefryn i oedd Claudette Colbert. Bette Davis a Joan Crawford oedd y Margedoedd uch Ifan.

*The stars at that time were William S. Hart, Lon Chaney and Chaplin, Paulette Goddard and Mae West, Laurel and Hardy, of course, and later Garbo and Gable. Also popular were Don Ameche, Barrymore, and Wallace Beery who depended more on his personality than his talent. He would be in films about the Bowery and the West, and once he played Pancho Villa. Beery was my favourite villain. My favourite film star was Claudette Colbert. Bette Davies and Joan Crawford were the viragos.*

**John E. Williams, Llanrug, Gwynedd**

Ffilm gyntaf y sinema newydd oedd addasiad cerddorol o stori Ali Baba a'r deugain o ladron, un yn dwyn yr enw tebyg i *Chu Chin Chow*. Dyma'r sinema a gyflwynodd Bette Davis, Errol Flynn, Joan Crawford, Greer Garson, Cary Grant, Gary Cooper, Spencer Tracy a Humphrey Bogart i bobol Stiniog. Dyma lle gwelais *Gone with the Wind* a hefyd *Kings Row*, ffilm wych gyda Ronald Reagan ynddi, heb fod yn gowboi. Mynd i weld *How Green Was My Valley* a dotio at ffurf oedd yn delynegol mewn du a gwyn prydferth. Aeth *Gone with the Wind* ddim i lawr yn rhy ffafriol yn Stiniog - un chwaer yn cyfeirio 'Wedi blino ar dymer ddrwg yr hen hogan yna ac yn rhy hir o lawer!' Ifan John yn breuddwydio am noswaith gyda Betty Grable, a Magi Puw yn dyheu am awr yng nghwmni Nelson Eddy. Jên Jôs yn dod allan drwy'r drws yn ddagrau i gyd ar ôl gweld *Wuthering Heights*: 'O Annie bach, fe fyddi wrth dy fodd yn hwn, enjoio pob munud, crïo o'r dechrau i'r diwedd!'

*The first film in the new cinema was a musical adaptation of Ali Baba and the Forty Thieves, titled something like* Chu Chin Chow. *This was the cinema that introduced Bette Davis, Errol Flynn, Joan Crawford, Greer Garson, Cary Grant, Gary Cooper, Spencer Tracy and Humphrey Bogart to the people of Blaenau Ffestiniog. That was where I saw* Gone with the Wind *and also* King's Row, *a superb film with Ronald Reagan in it, but not as a cowboy. I went to see* How Green Was My Valley, *and doted at its lyrical, beautiful, black and white form.* Gone with the Wind *didn't go down too well in Stiniog. One lady commented that she 'was fed up with that girl's bad temper, and it was much too long!' Ifan John dreaming about a night with Betty Grable, and Magi Puw longing for an hour in the company of Nelson Eddy. Jane Jones coming out through the door in tears after seeing* Wuthering Heights: *'Oh Annie bach, you'll love this one, you'll enjoy every minute, crying from beginning to end!'*

**Emyr Owen, Blaenau Ffestiniog, Gwynedd**

*War films were a major part of the programmes. We watched Errol Flynn fighting in the Far East, while John Mills, Michael Redgrave and Richard Todd played their parts in the Air Force and the Royal Navy. They made wonderful heroes with their stiff upper lips and their cut glass accents. We cried when Vivien Leigh threw herself under a*

# Swyn y Sêr
## *Film Idols*

*lorry for love in* Waterloo Bridge *and my mother enjoyed* Random Harvest *with Greer Garson so much that we must have gone every night that it was on that week. As girls our favourites were the musicals, although we did enjoy a good cry, sometimes. We watched Judy Garland and Mickey Rooney, Carmen Miranda, the Latin Bombshell, and we loved Alice Faye and Betty Grable. We all knew the scene where the handsome composer would sit at the piano tinkling the keys, with a beautiful young girl at his elbow, or draped enticingly along the top. Within minutes, he would have the inspiration for a song, she would pluck the lyrics out of thin air and, in no time at all, an invisible orchestra would be playing along in the background. And it all seemed perfectly reasonable to us. We even took Dracula and Frankenstein in our stride, although the loudest shout I have ever heard in any cinema, was that never-to-be-forgotten moment when Finlay Currie as Magwitch jumped out at Pip in the graveyard in* Great Expectations.

**Mrs Cora Edwards, ganed Treorci / born Treorchy**

*We always went to First House which started at 5.15 pm. and finished at eight. We would come out blinking after being in the dark for so long, and pass the queue for Second House. Then we'd go to Joe's and walk home eating our chips from salt-and-vinegar-soaked newspaper. Perhaps it was the printer's ink, but nowadays chips from plastic trays are nothing like as good. And we'd talk about Betty Grable, Rita Heyworth, Alice Faye and Carmen Miranda, Clark Gable, Spencer Tracy, Robert Taylor, Humphrey Bogart and Franchot Tone. And of course, Fred Astaire and Ginger Rogers.*

**Mrs Beryl Ellis, ganed / born Aberystwyth, Ceredigion**

*They all had their favourites - my mother was mad on Fredric March. Oh, if Fredric March was there, my mother would be there, and my stepsister, she was all James Mason... I used to like all the ugly ones - George Raft and James Cagney. I didn't like love stories, oh no! As long as it was blood and thunder, I was alright.*

**Mrs Peggy Page, Oakdale, Caerffili, ganed / born 1924**

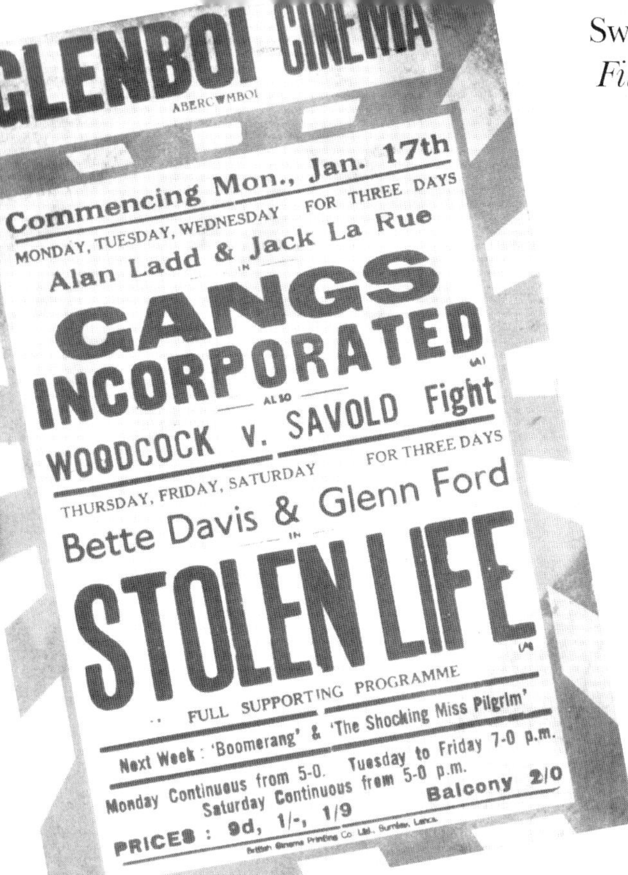


*I remember* Captains Courageous *with Freddie Bartholomew and Spencer Tracy. Freddie Bartholomew was a rich, spoilt little boy in it, and Spencer Tracy looked rough but he had a heart of gold, you know. And in the end he more or less gives his life for the boy. And the boy, because he had looked after him, turns out to be one of the best. I used to enjoy the tears. Then, when I was older, I used to enjoy Abbot and Costello. You'd have a really good laugh with Abbot and Costello.* Hold that Ghost - *I see it on the television now and it isn't the same.*

**Mrs Eirona Richards, Treforys / Morriston, ganed / born 1928**

Dyddiau braf iawn oedd hynny yn y 50s pan oeddwn yn dal i fynd i bictiwrs Pen-y-groes ar nos Fercher... Mynd yno ar ddydd Sadwrn i'r *matinée* i weld Roy Rogers, Gene Autry (y cowbois canu). Fy arwr i oedd Roy Rogers, a'i geffyl Trigger. Ar ôl inni dyfu i fyny, oeddan ni wedyn yn mynd ar nos Sadwrn i'r Majestic. Ew, dyna i chi *treat* - pob math o liwia a llyniau lliwiau! Roedd yna dri sinema yng Nghaernarfon: Majestic, Empire a Guild Hall. Ffug enw'r Guild Hall oedd *Laugh and Scratch*, ond yn y Guild Hall oedd y lluniau symud gorau. Yno welais i Doris Day gyntaf - roeddwn i wedi ei gweld hi yn canu ac actio *It's Magic* a *Calamity Jane*. Miwsic neis oedd yn y Guild Hall.

*They were wonderful days in the fifties when I used to go to the pictures in Pen-y-groes on a Wednesday night... I'd go there on a Saturday to the matinée to see Roy Rogers, Gene Autry (the singing cowboys). My hero was Roy Rogers and his horse Trigger. When we were older, we used to go to the Majestic on a Saturday night. Well, that was a treat - all kinds of colours and colour pictures! There were three cinemas in Caernarfon: the Majestic, Empire and Guild Hall. The Guild Hall's nickname was the Laugh and Scratch, but the Guild Hall had the best films. It was there that I first saw Doris Day - I saw her singing and acting in* It's Magic *and* Calamity Jane. *They used to have good music in the Guild Hall.*

**Mrs R. Thomas, Tal-y-bont, Gwynedd**

Gene Autry, un o'r 'cowbois canu', wedi rhoi benthyg ei het i Mrs Ruth Morris ar ymweliad â Chaerdydd, 1937.
*Gene Autry, 'The Singing Cowboy', lending his hat to Mrs Ruth Morris on a visit to Cardiff, 1937.*

## Sesiynau Sadwrn
## *The Penny Rush*

**Lee's Pictures, Menai Bridge**

**SPECIAL**

# Children's Matinees

**Every Saturday at 2-30.**

*My first memory of a visit to the pictures was going to the penny rush with my slightly older cousin on a Saturday morning. The penny rush was held in the Pavilion. There was nothing as sophisticated as an usherette. We had a man in charge who first of all kept us in control in the queue which snaked alongside the cinema. He would pounce on some unfortunate little boy saying, 'Didn't I throw you out of here last Saturday?' The answer as always, 'No, Mister, honest.' The poor man must have hated Saturday mornings. Once we were inside, he patrolled the aisles with a torch, flashing it in our faces while we tried to look innocent. Once the lights went off, the boys down in the front, who had paid a penny to get in, crawled their way under the seats through the various sweet papers, orange peel and dust to emerge from under the seats at the threepenny seats, looking as if they'd just come off a shift in the Park colliery...We thrilled to the adventures of Zorro, Flash Gordon and the Lone Ranger. The films were easier to understand then. The good guys were polite to the ladies and the villains wore the black hats. The Lone Ranger was obviously a gentleman, because he admonished the blokes on his side to 'aim for their wrists'. Before, you could say, 'Hey ho, Silver' we would be shouting encouragement at the good guys and screaming abuse at the crooks and the Indians. Tonto was the only good Indian that we knew in those unenlightened times. Fair play for the Red Man came along much later. Although we did not know how to play any game more complicated than Ludo, we sat on the edge of our seats if a poker game was in progress on the screen, and groaned at the turn of each card. The boys loved the gangster films and when they left the pictures they would talk like fugitives from the Bronx. Mrs. Johnson in the chip shop soon sorted them out though, when they asked her for 'Twopennorth of chips and easy on the vinegar'.*

**Mrs Cora Edwards, ganed Treorci / born Treorchy**

Palace Cinema, Aberhonddu, Powys, tua 1913.
*The Palace Cinema, Brecon, Powys, c. 1913.*

# Sesiynau Sadwrn
## *The Penny Rush*

Atgof ar ffurf darlun o fynedfa'r Plaza, Pen-y-groes, Gwynedd gan Mrs R.Thomas.

*A pictorial reminiscence of the foyer of the Plaza Cinema, Pen-y-groes, Gwynedd by Mrs R. Thomas.*

Gan mai chwarelwyr llechi oedd y rhan fwyaf o'n tadau, nid oedd llawer o gyfoeth o gwmpas, ac felly ein pres poced oedd ceiniog ar fore Sadwrn. Wedi cael y geiniog roedd ein criw yn cynnal pwyllgor i benderfynu sut oeddym yn mynd i wario'r geiniog, gan nad oedd un arall a'r gael tan y Sadwrn dilynol. Roedd dimau o dda-da, a chadw'r ddimau o newid a chael ychwaneg o dda-da dydd Llun neu ryw ben o'r wythnos nesaf, neu wario'r holl geiniog ar y Picshwrs yn y Blaenau yn y prynhawn, wedi cerdded tua milltir o'r ffordd i'r Sinema. Roedd y penderfyniad yn dibynnu yn aml ar y chwedl gyfres, gan y byddem yn aml yn chwara'r chwedl gyfres amser chwarae yn iard yr ysgol yr wythnos ganlynol os oedd yn gowbois ac Indiaid, neu rywbeth tebyg fel *The Red Glove*. Os wedi penderfynu ar y picshwrs, rhaid oedd wedyn drefnu amser cychwyn y cerddediad er mwyn i'r rhai ieuengach allu cadw i'r amser.

*As most of our fathers were slate quarrymen there wasn't much money about, so our pocket money would be a penny on Saturday morning. Once we had the penny, our gang would hold a committee meeting to decide how we were going to spend the penny, as there would be no more until the following Saturday. We'd spend a halfpenny on sweets and keep the halfpenny change for more sweets on Monday, or we'd spend the whole penny on the Pictures in Blaenau in the afternoon, after having walked the mile to the cinema. The decision depended very much on the serial, as we would re-enact the serial on the school yard the following week if it was cowboys and Indians or something similar, like* The Red Glove. *If we decided on the pictures, we'd have to arrange a time to start walking so that the younger ones could get there in time.*

**J.E. Pugh, Tanygrisiau, Gwynedd**

*The serial, I remember vividly, was called* Tailspin Tommy, *and as you can appreciate he was a pilot in a paper plane - it looked like paper anyway - and he was always going over either the sea or the volcanoes. When he came to the volcanoes, you'd see the plane coming lower and lower and the paper wings [would] start to burn. And when we're all going aaahh, it would say on the screen 'Continued next week'. He never went into the volcano, by the way. He never fell in the sea, but it was so exciting. And I must tell you also about this one particular occasion: they had a German film on. It was before the war. It was a silent film, and what they did for that particular film was they put miners lamps all around the Electric cinema. I can remember vaguely there was a lot of scenes underground with German miners. I can't tell you the plot of it because, you know, sitting at the back with a boy... but I do remember seeing all the lamps there and I do remember that they missed a lot of lamps. There was a hue and cry outside. They were searching the kids because some of the lamps had gone missing, but of course that's another story isn't it?*

**Mrs Iris Roderick Thomas, Merthyr Tudful, ganed / born 1927**

PEARL WHITE The screens most daring Serial Star in Ep. 9 of PLUNDER.
e latest and most sensational serial ever offered. Packed with exciting and thrilling incidents.

Cofiaf yr adeg dechreuais i fynd i'r pictiwrs (1928): 6c i seddau ôl a 3c i'r seddau blaen. Mi roedd yn well gweld y sgrîn fawr o'r seddau ôl - ffilmiau mud wrth gwrs. Rhai o'r seti blaen wedi cael eu cadw i'r ffyddloniaid: *Reserve Seats* am yr un pris. Rhyw hanner dwsin o'r merched selog yn y seddau ac yn mwynhau eu hunain yn fawr iawn ac yn cymeryd pob peth o ddifrif, yn enwedig y *Cowboys and Indians*. Ambell un yn gweiddi 'Watsha y cythral gwirion! Mae o y tu ôl i ti!' neu 'Sbïa! Dŵad wrtho fo!' Cofiaf un yn dweud ar ôl ffilm go gyffrous: 'Roeddan nhw yn ofnadwy heno yn lladd ei gilydd. Fydd 'na neb i wneud ffilm yn fuan!'

*I remember the time I started going to the pictures (1928): 6d for the back seats and 3d for the front. You could see the big screen better from the back seats - silent films of course. Some of the front seats were kept for the faithful: Reserve Seats for the same price. About half a dozen girls would be regularly in the seats, enjoying themselves tremendously and taking everything very seriously, especially the Cowboys and Indians. Some would shout 'Watch out you fool! He's behind you!' or 'Look! Tell him!' I remember someone saying after a particularly exciting film: 'They were awful tonight, killing each other. There'll be no-one left to make films soon!'*

**Hugh R. Jones, Llanberis, Gwynedd**

Hysbysebu ffa pob yn y Castle Cinema, Merthyr Tudful, 1950au.
*Promoting Heinz Baked Beans at the Castle Cinema, Merthyr Tydfil, 1950s*

# Sesiynau Sadwrn
## *The Penny Rush*

Cofiaf yn dda hefyd ffilmiau'r cyfresau, y *serials*. Beth bynnag oedd sefyllfa'r ferch dda neu'r filain drwg am chwarter i dri bob prynhawn Sadwrn, byddai'n sicr ddigon o ddod o'r sefyllfa anobeithiol. Nid a oedd o, neu hi, yn mynd i fyw diwrnod arall oedd y cwestiwn ar ddiwedd y prynhawn, ond SUT oedd o neu hi yn mynd i ddod o'r fath sitiwesion? Wedi'r cyfan roedd y llais anweledig o'r tu cefn yn gofyn yn ddigon plaen 'A ddaw eich arwr o hwn, yntau ai dyma'r diwedd?' Ond pwy ffŵl fuasai'n talu pedair ceiniog onibai fod y boi neu'r gyrl yn mynd i fyw am ddiwrnod arall? Os oedd y ferch wedi rhwymo rhwng y cledrau a golau pen arall i'r tynal, gellwch dderbyn gen i, nid trên arall sydd yna yn rhuthro i'w chyfeiriad, ond y boi gydag anferth o *flashlamp* yn dod i'w hachub. A dyma'r eiliad i guro traed a dwylaw.

*I remember the serials well. Whatever hopeless situation the heroine or the villain would be in at a quarter to three every Saturday afternoon, they were sure to get out of it. The question wasn't whether they were going to survive another day, but HOW were they going to get out of such a situation? At the end, the unseen voice at the back would ask quite plainly 'Will your hero escape, or is this the end?' But what fool would pay fourpence unless the boy or the girl was going to live another day? If the girl was tied to the railway tracks and a light appeared the other end of the tunnel, you can take it from me that it was not another train rushing in her direction, but the hero with a huge flashlamp coming to her rescue. And that was the moment for stamping our feet and clapping our hands.*

**Emyr Owen, Blaenau Ffestiniog, Gwynedd**

Roy Rogers a'i geffyl Trigger gan Mrs R. Thomas.
*Roy Rogers and his horse Trigger by Mrs R. Thomas.*

# Sesiynau Sadwrn
## *The Penny Rush*

*Mid Wales is not exactly the richest source for memories of going to the pictures, as cinemas were few and far between. One went over the border to Hereford for epics like* Gone with the Wind*! Now aged seventy-nine, I go back to the time when I was nine years old and an established 'Saturday Matinee' habitué queuing with our 'gang' for the (old) one penny seats. We usually clutched an orange or apple each, so necessary for throwing pips on the disdainful kids in the twopenny seats of the stalls below. We thrilled to watch Pearl White, the heroine of most of our films, being tied to the railway line in front of a fast approaching train; or Harold Lloyd or Buster Keaton in a 'Ford Tin Lizzie' being chased as he bounced over the level crossings. Music was very important to create the right atmosphere. My eldest sister being an accomplished pianist often helped with this. She spent much time synchronising her rallentando, fortissimo, accelerando and diminuendo with the films.*

**Mrs Marjorie Knowles, Llandrindod, Powys**

tgof darluniadol Mrs R. Thomas o'r Plaza, en-y-groes, Gwynedd.
*pictorial reminiscence by Mrs R.Thomas of the Plaza Cinema, en-y-groes, Gwynedd.*

*I suppose we started going to the pictures when I was seven or eight. We saw films like* Snow White*,* The Wizard of Oz *and all the Shirley Temple series. Then there were the cowboy films, with Roy Rogers and Trigger performing deeds of derring-do in the Wild West. And of course, the Saturday afternoon serials. The one I particularly remember was* Flash Gordon's Trip to Mars*, and every Saturday at 1.30 p.m. Mamgu, my brother John and I would walk to Aberystwyth through Plascrug, a tree-lined avenue used as a short cut by the people of Llanbadarn. There were thirteen episodes, and due to some dreadful circumstance, we were late leaving the house to go and see the very last. We hurried down through Plascrug, and as we neared the Station we could see the minute hand creeping inexorably towards the '12'. To my shame, I remember that we grabbed Mamgu's hands and made her run! And we got to the Coliseum just in time, puffing up the steps, the money ready in our hot little hands.*

**Mrs Beryl Ellis, ganed / born Aberystwyth, Ceredigion**

**Mon., Tues., Aug. 7—8 (U)**

ROY ROGERS in

**BELLS OF SAN ANGELO**

An amusing Western Comedy Drama you will enjoy.

**Also NOSON LAWEN**

The first full-length Welsh picture.

*Saturday mornings it was Buster Crabbe and Tom Mix and Roy Rogers and all those pictures. All of these pictures were always full. You'd be queuing up about quarter to ten in the morning, on a Saturday morning, to get in to the pictures... Mrs Badham was there then, she was the usherette, and of course we always used to go to the shop for a 'aporth of peanuts. And she'd say, 'Now you lot, before you go home you'll pick all them up and put them in your bag. Either take them home or hand them to me on your way out.' We would pick them up and drop them on the floor, you know how children are, but we always picked our shells up and give them back to her.*

**Mrs Peggy Page, Oakdale, Caerffili, ganed / born 1924**

*The Saturday morning matinées... held little attraction for me. By the mid to late 1960s the golden days of Saturday morning cinema were over - although there is much sentimental talk today about the matinée films, my recollection of Saturday morning cinema is that the main attractions were cigarettes and girls (in that order) and that little if any attention was paid to the screen! I suppose the peak of my cinema going must have been 1969 - 1972 (14-17 years), when I went to the cinema at least once and sometimes twice a week, especially in school holidays. Growing up in a small town, boredom was often a factor which drove me to the cinema, usually with as large a crowd of friends as could be mustered (17 of us went to see* Woodstock*). We would sometimes even go to see films we either knew little about or knew to be bad. The latter - usually horror movies, soft pornography or even Elvis films - would be mercilessly 'sent up' by heckling and general misbehaviour, often to the delight and amusement of the usually bored audience. When, as frequently happened, a film broke down or the projectionist put on the wrong reel, we would seize the opportunity to roar with mock rage, stamp our feet and hurl abuse at the apologetic manager, greeting his reassurances with ill mannered chants of 'money back', safe from all recognition in the darkness of the back rows. I cannot go to the cinema today without those chants ringing in my ears.*

**David Subacchi, ganed / born Aberystwyth, Ceredigion, 1955**

Aros i gael mynd i'r *matinée* yn y Capitol, Ystradgynlais, Powys, 1950au.
*Queuing for the matinée at the Capitol Cinema, Ystradgynlais, Powys, 1950s.*

# Y Seddau Cefn
## *The Back Row*

Gone with the Wind *was the nearest we ever came to having something obscene. Clark Gable carried her upstairs. I mean, you imagined the rest but that was enough. I mean, it was banned, wasn't it? He carried her upstairs, actually carried her upstairs, and we know what for. So that was banned. Today they're running around starkers and no-one blinks an eyelid, but that was the nearest I think they came to profanities or to having anything obscene on the stage. I mean, no woman would appear with a neckline that showed a little of her bosom. That would have to be covered up. There was no language. The nearest they came to a kiss, as you probably know, they used to kiss each other beneath the lips here. It looked as if they were kissing the lips, but they never did. They used to wander off under the light of the moon holding hands and you have to imagine the rest. There was never intimate scenes, bedroom scenes... I remember seeing Deanne Durbin and Robert Stack in the* The First Kiss *- Oh! we were swooning in the back, absolutely swooning! The boy I had with me wasn't very nice, but he was all right - he paid me in. But having said that, people behind you never bothered when you had a little smooch. Today they'd move you on and say go and sit in the back. Now the back row of the cinema was something different. First of all, you had to get in the queue early, because everybody in front were in couples and they were all trying to get in the back row of the cinema. To try and get out from there if you wanted to spend a penny, or you wanted to pop out and buy some nuts or something, was impossible because you were falling over everybody. Everybody was in a clinch - we used to call it smooching - and they were quite annoyed. I've had many swear words thrown at me in the back because I've tried to get out. 'Watch where you're going!' and 'What are you doing? If you want to move, don't sit in the back!' I think it was fourpence to sit in the back, but of course we never saw the film, did we? This was the awful thing. I'd come home ... and my mother'd say, 'Well, what did you see?' And I had to remember what it said on the outside of the cinema because you'd never remember. It was nothing serious. I mean, if a boy put his hand on your knee, he'd have a slap across the face, wouldn't he? All they got near to was a peck and a cuddle and a squeeze, but we thought that was most romantic.*

**Mrs Iris Roderick Thomas, Merthyr Tudful, ganed / born 1927**

Clark Gable a Vivien Leigh yn y ffilm *Gone With the Wind*, 1939.
*Clark Gable and Vivien Leigh in Gone With the Wind, 1939.*

# Y Seddau Cefn
## *The Back Row*

Och chi'n myn' miwn ar ddychre'r ffilm. Odd 'i ddim yn dywyll, *so* odd dim ishe *usherettes* a pithe fel'na, achos odd 'i'n ole. A we'ny, hanner awr 'di saith gwedwch, bydde'r gole i gyd yn myn' mâs. Ond cyn i'r gole fyn' mâs, odd sbri i gâl. Os odd bechgyn yn ishte yn y sete cefen, os ôn nw'n ffansïo ryw ferched, pelto nw â beth chi'n feddwl? Nage *roses*. Cnau mwncis! Os och chi'n câl ych pelto â cnau mwncis, och chi'n gwpod bod rywun yn ffansïo chi ta beth!

*You'd go in at the start of the film. It wasn't dark, so there was no need of usherettes and things like that, because it was light. And then at half past seven, all the lights would go out. But before they went out, there'd be a lot of fun. If there were boys sitting in the back row, and they fancied some of the girls, what do you think they'd pelt them with? Not roses. Monkey nuts! If you had monkey nuts thrown at you, at least you knew someone fancied you!*

**Mrs Peggy Jones, Brynaman, Sir Gaerfyrddin/ Carmarthenshire, ganed / born 1921**

*There was only one cloud on the horizon in the cinema as far as the female population was concerned. That was the wandering hand syndrome. It wasn't always the man in the greasy mac. On one occasion, I sat next to a man with his little girl on his knee who tried to give my knees a massage. Being a proper coward, I asked my friend in the next seat if she would change with me because I couldn't see. I won't repeat what she called me, but she had enough initiative to put her lighted cigarette on his hand. These creeps knew that most women would not make a fuss, but one evening I heard a woman shout at the top of her voice, 'Take your filthy hands off me, you dirty devil!' I admire her to this day.*

**Mrs Cora Edwards, ganed Treorci / born Treorchy**

# O Gochel y Sinema!
## *Beware of the Cinema!*

Dillad diwetydd a dillad dy' Sul. Odd dillad a dim ond dy' Sul odd reina i fod. Wath wi'n cofio fi'n mynd [i'r sinema] - 'Wel shgwl, ma'r 'en siwt fach 'na tipyn bach yn *shabby*. Cer â dillad gore heno nawr i'r Globe. Ond er mwyn y mawredd, newita nw pan dywi di nôl, streit, lle bo' dy dad-cu yn gweld nw. Wath O! Fydde fe'n gweud bo' ti'n mynd â siwt yr Ysbryd Glân at y diafol!'

*There were evening clothes and Sunday clothes. Some clothes you would only wear on a Sunday. Because I remember when I went [to the cinema] - 'Well look now, this suit has gone a bit shabby. Wear your best clothes tonight to the Globe. But for goodness' sake, change straight away when you get back, before your grandfather sees you. Because Oh! He'll say that you're taking the Holy Spirit's suit to the devil!'*

**D.E. Griffiths, Graig-cefn-parc, Abertawe / Swansea, ganed / born 1905**

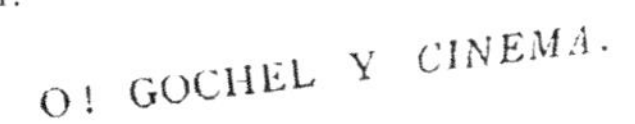
O! GOCHEL Y *CINEMA*.

I.

O! CADW fachgenyn O'r *Cinema* ddu:
Mae rhwyd gan y gelyn, Dan flodyn, a phlu,
Athrofa drygioni, Yw'r *Cinema'n* wir—
Mae'n lladd pob daioni, Sy'n codi'n y tir.

II.

Erch fwystfil ac Angel, Yng ngh'lonnau plant sydd,
A rhyngddynt mae'n rhyfel—P'run garia y dydd?
Bwystfilod mawr, cethin, O'r *Cinema* gwyd!
I'r Angel, i'w feithrin, O! hogyn, rho fwyd.

III.

Y 'deryn 'sglyfaethus, A bwystfil y ffôs,
Sy'n teithio'n fradwrus, Dan lenni y nos;
Wrth fynd ar yr Oriel, Fe ddywed y Llun—
Tu cefn, yn y dirgel, Mae'r Diafol ei hun!

IV.

Mae dyn gyda'r Diafol, Mewn cyngrair, yn hon—
Dyn call—nid urddasol, Ond aur ar ei fron!
Y dyn ddwêd wrth Satan—" O elw y Llun,
Cymeraf fi'r Arian, Cei dithau y Dyn!"

V.

Y gwaetha' o uffern, A goreu y byd,
Osoda y Gethern, Mor gyfrwys, yng nghyd:
Yn Llestri Tŷ'r Arglwydd, Rhoir grawnwin y Fâll!
I'r anfad waradwydd, Mae'r werin yn ddâll!

Darn o gerdd gan Y Parch. Thomas David Evans (Gwernogle), 1939.
*A few verses of an anti-cinema poem by the Rev. Thomas David Evans (Gwernogle), 1939.*

Yr ymgyrch i agor sinemâu ar y Sul - Sinema'r Castle, Merthyr Tudful, 1956.
*The Sunday screening campaign at the Castle Cinema, Merthyr Tydfil, 1956.*

# AGOR SINEMAU AR Y SUL

UN o'r problemau sydd wedi codi allan o'r rhyfel ac sydd yn peri peth penbleth i Gymru mewn llawer lle yw'r un ynglŷn â'g agor sinemau ar y Sul.

Y Cymro, 13/1/1940

# O Gochel y Sinema!
## *Beware of the Cinema!*

*There were two landmarks in Morriston, the Regal Cinema and Tabernacle. Now Tabernacle with its big spire and the Regal, it had a large front and on top was a big dome with Mercury standing on top of the dome. And you could see it for miles... . My grandmother very rarely went to the cinema. I took her once to the Regal to see Fredric March in* One Foot in Heaven. *That was because it was a story of a minister. And when they were playing a hymn on a harpsichord in it, I had a job to keep her from starting to sing. But everything else, if there was a kiss or a cuddle, it would be* 'Ych a fi!' *My mother and father liked the pictures, and my uncle* **lived** *in the pictures. When I used to go and play upstairs... with my dolls, I was taking them to chapel in my grandmother's room, and taking them into my uncle's room, I was taking them to the pictures. [I thought I was] desecrating my grandmother's room if I was taking them to the pictures in my grandmother's room.*

**Mrs Eirona Richards, Treforys / Morriston, ganed / born 1928**

*Most of our neighbours were Chapel, and frowned on the fleshpots. We were Church of Wales, however, and consequently flighty, and although they disapproved of us they were pleased to let us mind their children for an hour or two in the picture house.*

**Mrs Beryl Ellis, ganed / born Aberystwyth, Ceredigion**

*It was the old Biblical quote: Sunday was made for man, not man made for Sunday. In those days, Sunday was sacrosanct. I mean that was like a special day. I can go along with it being a day of rest, but not having films or cinemas open was a bit excessive.*

**Paul Barrett, Penarth, ganed / born 1941**

Yr ymgyrch i agor sinemâu ar y Sul, Merthyr Tudful, 1956.
*The Sunday screening campaign, Merthyr Tydfil, 1956.*

**Police loud-speaker warned thousands more —"No hope"**

ONE brief hour sufficed for the holding of the mu publicised town meeting of electors in Brangwyn Hall last night to accept or reject the p posal that cinemas should be open in Swansea Sundays. The hall was packed, and the voting v decisive in so far as those who managed to get into hall were concerned.

**They rejected the proposal by 1,411 votes to after six speeches had been made, three for ar three against the proposal, and each of only fiv minutes' duration.**

As the Mayor, Alderman W. G. Rees, declar the meeting closed, a large section of the crowd bro into the hall singing "Onward, Christian Soldier then "Calon Lan."

Erthygl yn y *South Wales Evening Post*, 20 Hydref, 1950, yn sôn am gyfarfod yn Neuadd Brangwyn, Abertawe, i bleidleiso ynglyn ag agor sinemâu ar y Sul.
*An article from the South Wales Evening Post, 20 October, 1950, reporting on a meeting held in the Brangwyn Hall, Swansea, to vote on Sunday screenings.*

# Llygad ar y Byd
## *A Window on the World*

*You'd have all the news The British Movietone News you know, the films saying 'Costs Lives' and all that, and the blackout and that sort of thing. But I remember in the 1930s... during the coronation of King George the Sixth, all the schools in Morriston were marched to the Regal and we saw the film of the coronation. And we sang Coronwch Ef yn ben. Coronwch, coronwch, coronwch Ef yn ben, all the way to the Regal to see the Coronation film.*

**Mrs Eirona Richards, Treforys / Morriston, ganed / born 1928**

Un nos Sadwrn y plant yn gorfod mynd allan i'r cyntedd yn y Forum. Roedd y ffilmiau bychan oedd yn cynnal y rhaglen wedi bod, ac yn groes i'r arfer cadwyd y ffilm newyddion tan o flaen y brif ffilm. Y rheswm am hyn oedd ffilm o newyddion arbennig yn dangos mewn gryn fanyldeb milwyr Prydain, Rwsia, a'r Unol Daleithiau yn rhyddhau trueiniaid Belsen a'r gwersylloedd uffernol arall. Y ffilm y noswaith hon oedd *The White Cliffs of Dover.* Credwch neu beidio, fe gollwyd mwy o ddagrau yn ystod y darlun hwn nag yn ystod y ffilm o'r gwersylloedd annynol!

*One Saturday night the children had to go out to the foyer in the Forum. The short films which supported the programme had finished, and contrary to the norm, the news film was kept until before the main feature. The reason for this was a special news film showing in much detail soldiers from Britain, Russia and the United States releasing the poor people from Belsen and the other hellish camps. The film that night was* The White Cliffs of Dover. *Believe it or not, there were more tears lost during that picture than during the film of the inhuman concentration camps!*

**Emyr Owen, Blaenau Ffestiniog, Gwynedd**

Sleidiau llusern a ddefnyddid ar gyfer hysbysebu rhwng ffilmiau mewn sinema yn Saundersfoot, Penfro.

*Lantern slide used as advertisements between features in a cinema in Saundersfoot, Pembrokeshire.*

*Pre-television you see. The Pathé news. We saw what was happening in other parts of the world. That was our only way of seeing it. I can still see the the news report of the siege of Stalingrad. I can see that on the film now. On black and white. And the landings, Normandy and all the rest of it and how the progress of the war was going on. We were shown the maps. But Pathé news was the only one we had. We never saw it apart from the papers, which we never read as kids.*

**Tom Davies, Oakdale, Caerffili, ganed / born 1932**

*France surrendered to the Germans and the Germans occupied the whole of France... and every cinema and every public building in this country was shut for a week. And 'till the end of the week the public thought the end of the war was here, that we were losing the war. Everybody was depressed and nothing to do and we had a message then. 'Open as soon as you can', everything in the town, so we had to rush everything open then.*

*You'd be surprised at the attitude of the public with no cinemas and nothing to do. There was no television then of course.*

**Arthur Austin, peiriannydd cinema Abertawe / cinema engineer Swansea, ganed / born 1903**

*The War, the Second World War that is, didn't close the cinemas. They flourished with a bigger audience of soldiers and airmen who came to train in Aberystwyth, and eventually with Yanks, American soldiers relieving their home-sickness by hearing American scenes and food. I remember once, during one of the early Forties musicals, Betty Grable, in glorious technicolour, fried some bacon and eggs. This was at the time when Britons were receiving rations of one rasher of bacon and one egg per week, and when she dropped them in to the frying pan, and they made that delicious sizzling noise, the whole audience went 'Ahhhhh' with nostalgia for pre-1939 plenty.*

**Mrs Beryl Ellis, ganed / born Aberystwyth, Ceredigion**

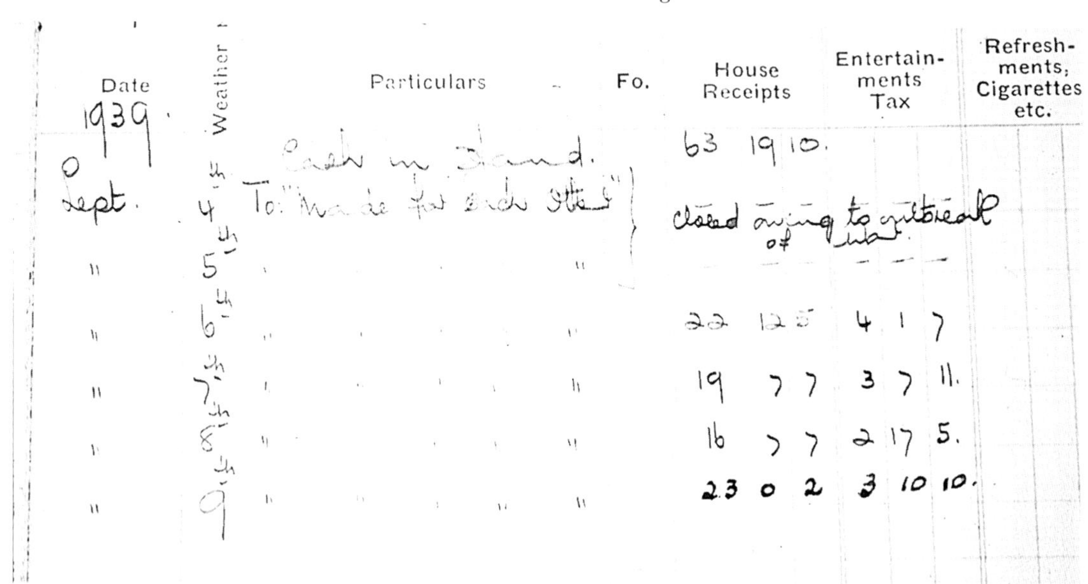

| Date | Weather | Particulars | Fo. | House Receipts | Entertainments Tax | Refreshments, Cigarettes etc. |
|---|---|---|---|---|---|---|
| 1939 | | Cash in Hand. | | 63 19 10. | | |
| Sept. | 4th | To: "Made for each other" | | closed owing to outbreak of war | | |
| " | 5th | " | " | | | |
| " | 6th | " | " | 22 12 5 | 4 1 7 | |
| " | 7th | " | " | 19 7 7 | 3 7 11. | |
| " | 8th | " | " | 16 7 7 | 2 17 5. | |
| " | 9th | " | " | 23 0 2 | 3 10 10. | |

Cofnod yn llyfr lóg y Coliseum, Aberystwyth, am gau'r sinema ar ddau ddiwrnod cyntaf y rhyfel, Medi 1939.
*An entry in the log book of the Coliseum Cinema, Aberystwyth, recording the closure of the cinema on the first two days of war, September 1939.*

Ymgyrch gyhoeddusrwydd i gydfynd â dangos y ffilm *High Society* yn sinema'r Castle, Merthyr Tudful, 1956.

*Publicity stunt to coincide with the showing of High Society at the Castle Cinema, Merthyr Tydfil, 1956.*

*They used to have fashion shows on the stage from the different clothiers. I remember one ladies' boutique was called Weston Gowns, and they'd have all the assistants parading in the latest wear. Then there was a hypnotist. I remember seeing, a live hypnotist on stage there, and of course when Shirley Temple films came out we had our Shirley Temple in Merthyr Tydfil. We had about twenty of them. They were all on the stage this particular day - you know, little pretty dresses with red spots, big bows, cork screw curls, all doing their best. Two of them they were exceptionally good. They really looked like Shirley Temple. I think one of them was called Margaret Thomas and she lived not far from where I lived in Bailey Glas Court, and the other one was called Norma Price and she lived on the way down to the Temperance Hall. It was very difficult to choose between them. I think they both had first prize. You see, it wasn't just a cinema with films.*

**Mrs Iris Roderick Thomas, Merthyr Tudful, ganed / born 1927**

*Shirley Temple dresses were a small frock, gathered at the yoke and buttoned through. And little white collars and floral you know. Oh you thought you were cheese if you had Shirley Temple dresses. Then you had all the musicals: Betty Grable musicals and all the big bands and things then. And with all the big bands you were learning jitterbugging. De dede de de dede de- de. Only hear that and I'd be off. 'In the Mood'...You'd go to the films and when you come home you copy what you see on the films.That was why we could dance the jitterbug as good as anybody, just by seeing them in the films, and of course everybody used to do their hair like the film actresses. We didn't see all the fashions on paper in those times - you saw them all in the cinema. What film actresses did, you did. You'd try to do your hair the same as them, up in quiffs in the front, pageboy in the back, that sort of thing.*

**Mrs Eirona Richards, Treforys / Morriston, ganed / born 1928**

*James Dean, like he had a red jacket, I wanted a red jacket. Marlon Brando had a leather jacket, I want a leather jacket, that kind of thing. But I think there was a cut-off time then, because I really wanted a hat like Humphrey Bogart. But I mean I'm 16 or 17 and there's no way I can go round with a trilby on, as much as I wanted to, so I never did the trilby. But it was the cinema and what was happening... . When* Rock Around the Clock *was shown in the cinemas - if you see the film now it's very innocuous - but at the time it was a huge sensation and everyone from magistrates to Tory backbenchers were flipping out and blaming everything on this film. And it was banned in certain areas. But they showed it at the Windsor cinema in Penarth. They wouldn't show it at the Washington, but they would show it at the Windsor. And I went and we were in there with the kids in the cheap seats. This would be [19]56, so I'd be 15. But what I was aware of, the adults were in the more expensive seats - obviously come to watch what the kids were going to do, you see. So when the music started playing (and I don't really know if it was because it was expected of us and that might have been part of it, but it really was a genuine excitement with the music), I can remember getting up and dancing about in the aisle. In fact when I was jiving in the aisle, I found out I was jiving with a man called Bugsy Barnes. I couldn't find a girl in the struggle. But it was a very good-natured sort of disturbance and everybody seemed quite pleased really. The parents all had something to tut tut about and the kids had a bop, so it was a good night for one and six.*

**Paul Barrett, Penarth, ganed / born 1941**

*Everyone went to see* Proud Valley. *But when we all went to see the film* How Green Was My Valley, *it was a very sad film but you took it all with a pinch of salt, 'specially when you saw her outside the door with her pinafore catching all the men's wages when they went in. You knew the mother would be looking after the money in the house, but she wouldn't be outside with her*

Dawnsio roc a rôl mewn cystadleuaeth ym Mhenarth, 1950au.

*Rocking and rolling in a dance competition, Penarth 1950s.*

How Green Was My Valley, 1941

*pinafore, and the colliers wouldn't be singing all the way home from work, you know what I mean. We knew that wasn't right, and yet we took what they did in America as gospel. Of course, we thought America was marvellous. And when the Americans came over here then, we thought they were all the same as on the films. We didn't think of the poor parts of America.*

**Mrs Eirona Richards, Treforys / Morriston, ganed / born 1928**

*America was what I admired and all my contemporaries did, because really for Britain... you had the damn class system. All you could look up to was Kenneth More, nice Kenneth More, patches on his jacket, like, cap and all that. But I mean he belonged to that class, you know. Bloody brogue shoes - give me a break! So it was America that was classless and America that was cool. I can remember thinking it would be great to drink Coca Cola, and yet when it first came into Wales, I remember going to Cardiff market and buying it and drinking it from the bottle and thinking, this is fabulous, this is like being at some drive-in or somewhere, but oh it wasn't. But yeah they all had the cool stuff and all the good things you wanted to be part of... I do know that a lot of people, when we were kids, would talk about going to America. I can remember these girls talking about going to America to meet Elvis but they weren't sure where he lived, if he lived in Hollywood or if he lived in Memphis or if he lived in Hawaii. So there was like debates of where to go and all that stuff. I think it was more of an impossible dream... There was just no need to go to America. America came to us.*

**Paul Barrett, Penarth, ganed / born 1941**

Marlon Brando yn y ffilm *The Wild One*, 1954
*Marlon Brando in The Wild One, 1954*

# Cyfaredd y Cysgodion
## *The Dream House*

*It was wonderful experience really because it was a bit of a fantasy thing. Life wasn't all that marvellous, obviously, with one thing and another, so this took you out of the reality of life as it was.*

**Jim Cowley, Caerdydd / Cardiff, ganed / born 1927**

Wrth i'r perchennog gau'r llenni, cauwyd hefyd glaw a llaithder Stiniog o'r tu allan ac o'r cof. Credaf fod atebiad yma i resymeg adloniant y cysgodion. Hen frodorion Stiniog, cynefin â'r llwch a llafur caled, yn cael cyfle i anghofio'r bywyd go-iawn drwy weld y llenni'n cau ar y byd y tu allan a llenni'r sinema'n agor ar fywyd moethus a llawn haul Holiwd.

*As the proprietor shut the curtains, the rain and dampness of Stiniog was also shut outside and out of our minds. I believe that this was the reason behind the appeal of this entertainment of the shadows. The old inhabitants of Stiniog, who were used to dust and hard labour, had the opportunity to forget the real world by seeing the curtains shut on the world outside and the cinema curtains opening on the luxurious, sunny world of Hollywood.*

**Emyr Owen, Blaenau Ffestiniog, Gwynedd**

*You could go to the cinema and really be transported into a world that was a million miles away from the one you dwelt in... When I went to the cinemas and saw the films I could be as grown up as you like and I could drink whisky and smoke Lucky Strike and wear a big raincoat or whatever, you know, drive fast cars and cavort with blondes, anything.*

**Paul Barrett, Penarth, ganed / born 1941**

Blaenau Ffestiniog, 1933

# Cyfaredd y Cysgodion
## *The Dream House*

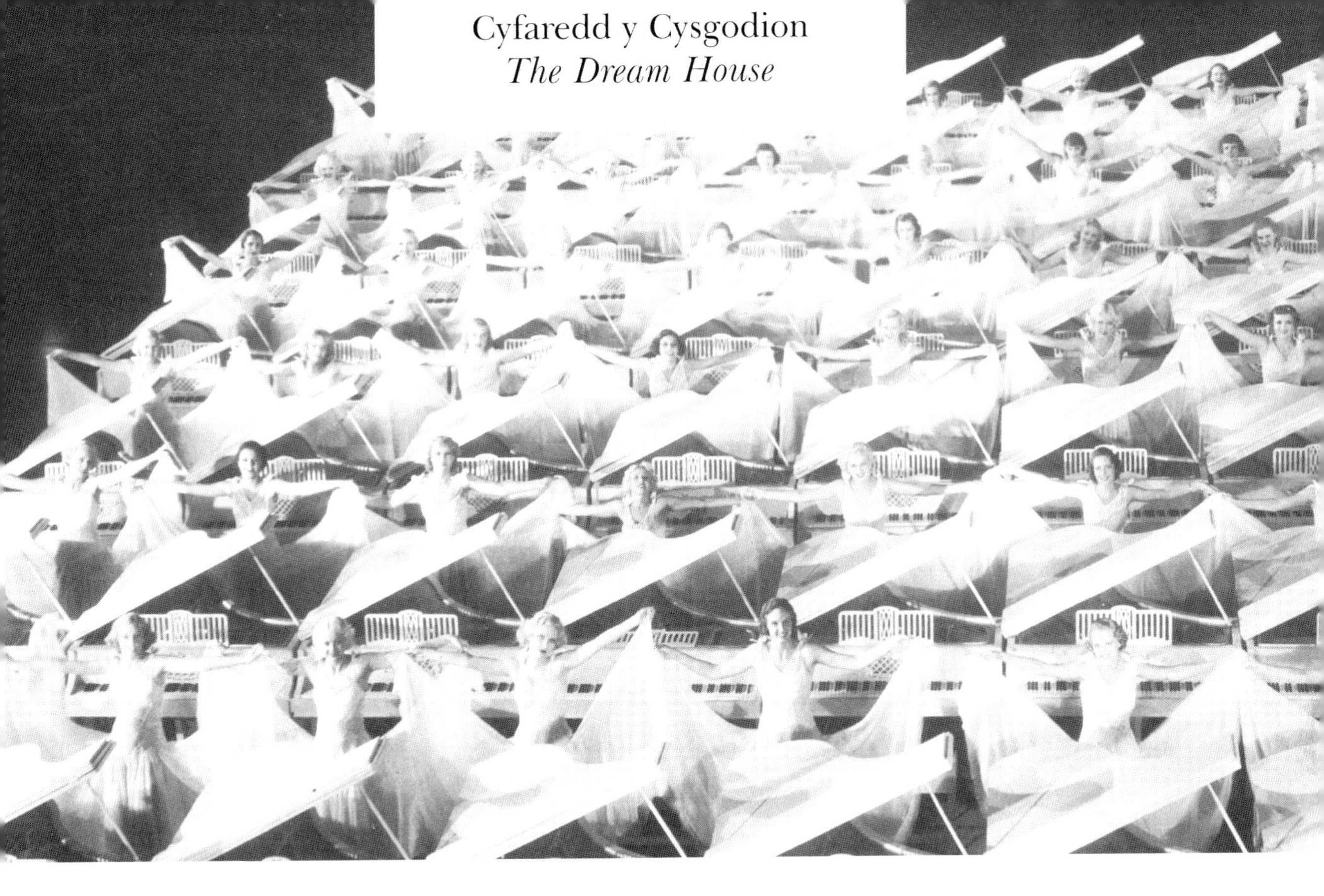

Byd ffantasi Hollywood yn y ffilm *Gold Diggers of 1935*

*The fantasy world of Hollywood in the film* Gold Diggers of 1935

Am bris dwy geinog och chi'n gallu mynd mâs o'r probleme - dim arian, dim llawer o ddillad, ddim gallu mynd i unman tu fâs i'r pentre - a chi'n myn' i fyd glittering Hollywood. Odd y shews ôn nw'n dangos - *musicals* ôn i'n lico fwya', â'r *chorus girls* a'r *lines* a'r *plumes* mawr ar 'u penne, a cico'u coese lan. Wel, chi'n gwbod, och chi'n galler anghofio pethe. Wi'n cretu ta mynd i'r sinema ôn nw i anghofio pethe.

*For tuppence you could leave the problems - no money, not many clothes, not being able to go anywhere outside the village - and enter the glittering world of Hollywood. The shows that they used to put on - I liked musicals most of all, with the lines of chorus girls and big plumes on their heads. And do you know, you could forget about things. I think they went to the cinema to forget.*

**Mrs Peggy Jones, Brynaman, Sir Gaerfyrddin /Carmarthenshire, ganed / born 1921**

*There was nothing else to do, you see, only go to the cinema. I didn't drink, I didn't smoke - that was the life.. It was the cinema, and there [were] so many films on you could see a different film every night of the week if you wanted to. And it was a community place. It was exciting really. It was fun going. You'd have a chat, and you were amongst people. I think human beings have got to be amongst people. That's what keeps you young.*

**Vincent Thomas, Merthyr Tudful, ganed / born 1927**

# O Balasau i Bingo
# *From Dream Palace to Bingo*

COUNTY THEATRE
BANGOR Telephone: 2828
Matinees Wed. & Thurs. 2.15. Doors Open Nightly 5 o'clock.

This Friday and Saturday. Continuous from 5.30.
Cary Grant, Loretta Young: THE BISHOP'S WIFE.
Laurel and Hardy: LIVE GHOSTS

MONDAY, NOV. 6th. At 7.30. Doors open 6.30

**BINGO CLUB NIGHT**

You must be a member for 24 hours before you can play.
Each member allowed two guests.

**BIG CASH PRIZES**

MAKE THIS YOUR NIGHT OUT. JOIN NOW!
It's Exciting! It's Terrific! It's a Grand Night Out!

Bellach, does yr un sinema yn Blaenau Ffestiniog. Mae'r hen Empire yn siop ddodrefn ers blynyddoedd. Does dim ond tŷ neu ddau lle bu sinema'r Parc, ac mae'r Forum yn eiddo Kwiks hefyd ers blynyddoedd bellach... Gwelsom lawer ffilm yn gorffen gyda golygfa o'r arwr a'r eneth gariadus yn marchogaeth i gyfeiriad y gorwel a'r machlud haul. Erbyn hyn mae'r sinemâu wedi gwneud yr un fath yn union.

*Nowadays there are no cinemas in Blaenau Ffestiniog. The old Empire has been a furniture shop for years. There is only a few houses where the Park cinema used to be... and the Forum has been in Kwiks' hands for years... We saw many films finishing with a scene of the hero and his sweetheart riding off into the sunset. By now, the cinemas have done exactly the same*

**Emyr Owen, Blaenau Ffestiniog, Gwynedd**

*All three cinemas have now closed. The Pier Cinema is a Bingo Hall, the Coliseum, rightly, a museum, and the Forum a car park. Today's children are prevented from attending today's violent, sexually explicit films. Only Stephen Spielberg seems to understand about entertainment. We saw nearly every film made, and it was richness indeed.*

**Mrs Beryl Ellis, ganed / born Aberystwyth, Ceredigion**

Sinema'r Coliseum, Treganna, Caerdydd, 1986.
*The Coliseum Cinema, Canton, Cardiff, 1986*

Kenneth Scott yn gweithio peiriannau sinema y Forum, Blaenau Ffestiniog, am y tro diwethaf yn 1970.
*Kenneth Scott, the projectionist at the Forum Cinema, Blaenau Ffestiniog, using the equipment for the last time in 1970.*

# O Balasau i Bingo
## *From Dream Palace to Bingo*

Doedden ni ddim yn sylweddoli ar y pryd, ond yr oedd hyn oll yn ddechreuad tranc adloniant syml cefn gwlad. Daeth y sinemâu yn ffordd o fyw ac yn is-ddiwylliant. Adloniant oedd prif bwrpas y ffilmiau, er efallai bob pedwar amser ceid ffilm am deithio. Heddiw mae'r Guild Hall wedi ei chau a'i selio. Ers dim llawer roedd yna ryw hen foi rhonc a'i gefn ar y drws yn dweud wrthyf mewn cyfrinach mawr, *'This place used to be a cinema you know'*. Cwt Bingo yw'r Empire a dim ond plisgen yw'r Majestic, ei thu mewn yn lludw ar ôl y tân a ddechreuwyd yn fwriadol. Mae'r oll oeddent yn ei arlwyo a mwy ar gael wrth y tân heddiw; bendith fawr i un tros oed yr addewid fel fi, ond mae'n ffwl preis i dalu am golli cymdeithasgarwch y Guild Hall ar nos Sadwrn.

*We didn't realise it at the time, but all of this was the beginning of the end for simple rural entertainment. The cinema became a way of life and a sub-culture. The main purpose of the films was entertainment, though you had the odd travel film. Now the Guild Hall has been closed and boarded up. Not long ago a lad leaning against the door told me in great secrecy, 'This place used to be a cinema, you know.' The Empire is a Bingo Hall, and the Majestic only a shell, its interior in ashes after the fire which had been lit deliberately. All that they offered and more is available today by the fireside; a great blessing for someone over the promised age like myself, but it's full price to pay for losing the sense of community in the Guild Hall on a Saturday night.*

**John E. Williams, Llanrug, Gwynedd**

Hen sinema'r Empire, Caernarfon, Gwynedd, bellach yn Neuadd Bingo.
*The former Empire Cinema, Caernarfon, Gwynedd, now the Appollo Bingo Club.*

Sinema'r Majestic, Caernarfon, Gwynedd, 1990au.
*The Majestic Cinema, Caernarfon, Gwynedd, 1990s.*

Newydd Wedd

*A New Image*

*I forgot all about this, about how wonderful it was to go to cinemas, until three weeks ago. I happened to go with my husband on a day's outing... and all of a sudden we could see a big poster,* THE ODEON NOW SHOWING, *and it was the new Walt Disney film. It was* The Lion King *and you see not knowing these things I went to the front desk and I said to the girl 'I'll have two seats in the circle,' and I said, 'What do they cost?' and she said 'They're four pound ninety five.' I nearly had a blue fit... because the last thing I saw was* Ben Hur *and I thought 'Oh! Four pound ninety five!' 'OK,' I said, 'I'll have two.' So she showed me this chart and I picked two seats, of course not knowing about the latest procedures. There were three different studios there, but* The Lion King *was in the main studio with the bi-screen it said. So I followed the signs, I got up stairs, and I'm by the door with my husband. I opened the door and a face pops out and this woman says to me, 'What do you want?'.And I said, 'I've come to see the film. We've got tickets.' 'Oh no, my dear,' she said, 'You can't see the film now, you have to wait until the house is emptied. You'll have to wait three quarters of an hour.' I said, 'Oh I don't mind. I'll come in and I'll wait.' She said 'You can't wait for the performance to finish and sit through it. You have to stand in the queue at the bottom of the stairs and then we'll call you up.' Well, for the very first time I realised what a change there had been from the time that I was young. Everything was done in order - stand, queue, call, sit where we put you, you will really laugh where we want you to laugh. I thought this isn't the home that we used to go to where we'd take our cheese sandwiches and slices of rice pudding. My mother used to make rice pudding that was solid, you see, and I used to cut it into squares and take it with me to the cinema. I thought, well, these days are gone. I could never sit here eating rice pudding nor chewing nuts because I'd be thrown out. But I could have done it years ago in the Electric.*

**Mrs Iris Roderick Thomas, Merthyr Tudful, ganed/ born 1927**

# Multi-screen cinema plan

By Victoria Ellis

A NEW five-screen cinema could regenerate the top end of the High Street, if planners vote to allow major renovations to Bangor's Plaza cinema.

Apollo, who own the cinema and 16 others throughout the country, have plans to extend the Plaza to provide five screens, instead of the two already there.

The £1.2m renovation involves building a new all-glass entrance and foyer area.

chief planning officer Gwyn Hughes back the plans which will go before Arfon planning committee in two weeks.

"It's brilliant as we really do need the extra screens in Bangor," said Mrs Tilman.

"So often in the past we have missed out on good films because if there are several movies on the circuit and we only have two screens, we just have to

## Shops will have to be razed

further down the High Street.

"If people do park at that end and walk the short distance to the cinema, it could trigger a regeneration

Rhan o erthygl yn y *Bangor and Anglesey Mail*, Mawrth 1995.

*An extract from an article printed in the* Bangor and Anglesey Mail, *March 1995.*

# Newydd Wedd
## *A New Image*

Sinema Institiwr y Gweithwyr, Coed Duon, ar ei newydd wedd, 1990au.

*A new image at the cinema of Blackwood Miners' Institute, 1990s.*

Cwsmeriaid cyntaf sinema newydd y Pafiliwn, Porthcawl, Gorffennaf 1994.

*First customers at the box office of the new Grand Pavilion Cinema, Porthcawl, July 1994.*

# I barhau...?
# *To be continued...?*

KING
KONG
LET